THE GEEK'S GUIDE

JOB HUNTING

CRANE HILL
PUBLISHERS

ISBN-13: 978-1-57587-259-9
ISBN-10: 1-57587-259-5

Design by Miles G. Parsons

Printed in the United States

Library of Congress Cataloging-in-Publication Data

Beam, Linda J.
   Geek's guide to job hunting / Linda J. Beam.
     p. cm.
   ISBN-13: 978-1-57587-259-9
   1. Job hunting. 2. Employment interviewing. 3. Résumés
(Employment) 4. Vocational guidance.   I. Title.
   HF5382.7B376 2006
   650.14--dc22

2006031144

THE GEEK'S GUIDE
JOB HUNTING

Linda J. Beam

CRANE HILL
PUBLISHERS

CONTENTS

Help for the Hunt 7

In the Beginning 9

Seek and Ye Shall Find 23

Roadmap for Résumés 39

Missive with a Mission 57

Signed, Sealed, Delivered.. 65

Getting Ready for Your Close-up 77

Dressing for Impressing... 85

Hey, Look Me Over 95

When Opportunity Knocks....................................... 115

Yes, No, or Maybe 123

It's Not Easy Being Green 129

Corporate Courtesies.. 135

Index 157

THE GEEK'S GUIDE

HELP FOR THE HUNT

Whether you are new to the job market, or are just looking for a change, job hunting can seem daunting. It's not just finding job opportunities; it's also getting the attention of those in charge of hiring, landing the all-important interview, and then clinching the offer! All that, while you keep an eye on other qualified candidates trying to overtake you in the race for the perfect job. No doubt about it, the job market is competitive. You'll need an edge.

That's where *The Geek's Guide to Job Hunting* can help. From the day you begin your search, to the day you begin your job, it offers practical advice every step of the way. Whether you need pointers about where to look for job prospects, or you need to know what to wear to an interview, this book has it all.

But it doesn't leave you there. It helps you transition from being a job seeker to an employee by offering tips on how to get off on the right foot, and then how to become a considerate co-worker in addition to being a skilled one.

IN THE BEGINNING

As you lay the groundwork for a successful job search, there are some important decisions to be made. You have to have a plan.

Not only will developing a plan get you to your ultimate goal of landing a job, but in the meantime, it will help relieve anxiety about what you should be doing next by providing a step-by-step outline for you to follow.

1. Take inventory. Before you start to look for a job, you have to know what kind of job you're looking for. You'll want to identify the right job for you.

GEEK*Speak:*

"Those who fail to plan, plan to fail."
Unknown

The first step in identifying your job should be to analyze your abilities and interests. There are many factors that play into this: your interests, your personality, and even your hobbies might be good indicators of the job you should do.

Identifying your skills is a critical beginning because it not only helps you identify the right job for you, it will also help you pinpoint what you have to offer an employer.

If you've just finished college, you might reasonably assume that your dream job will be related to your course of study. But some people decide to go in other directions, so take time to think seriously about this.

GEEK*Speak:*

Don't let other people's opinions determine what job you should pursue. Suppose Elvis Presley had listened to Jim Denny, manager of the *Grand Ole Opry*, following the young singer's first performance there: "You ain't goin' nowhere...son. You ought to go back to driving a truck."

Make as objective a list as possible of skills that you've obtained through your education, activities, and life experiences. Nothing is too small to be considered.

Here are some questions you may ask yourself to help you begin:

- What subjects interest you? That sounds like an obvious question, but there's no sense taking a job in a field where you have no aptitude or interest.

- Do you already have training in a particular area? For instance, if you have a college degree, or have taken extra classes, consider putting that education to use.

GEEK**OID**

Listing skills may sound like an easy thing to do, but because you are not objective about yourself, it may be difficult. To begin, think about any job you've had, even as a volunteer. List the duties you did in that job, and you have the beginning of your list. Another way to jumpstart your list is to think of classes you've had in which you learned to do something new, and list what it was.

GUERRILLA GEEK

There are many ways to evaluate your skills. Career counseling services at local universities and community colleges often offer career testing which will translate your likes and dislikes into relevant vocational options. Aptitude tests reveal your ability to do certain types of work well. Personality tests reveal characteristics that make you suitable for particular jobs.

 *Even if you intend to work within your major, stay open to other possibilities so you don't overlook a good job.*

- What is your personality? Are you thoughtful and attentive to details, or are you creative?

- What are your hobbies? Perhaps you should look for a job doing something at which you already excel. Maybe you could even teach your special interest to others.

When you think about skills, identify those that are actual job skills (typing, computer expertise), as opposed to soft skills (people skills).

- Do you enjoy working with other people, or do you prefer more solitary endeavors?

GUERRILLA GEEK

If you have no idea at all what kind of job you'd like, here's a very low-tech way to get some direction: keep a career diary. Keep a notebook of things that interest you. If you see a newspaper article that describes a job you'd enjoy, write it down. If you see an ad on TV that prompts an idea, write it down.

Look over what you've written, and see if you can detect a pattern that would indicate the perfect job for you!

- Do you have leadership abilities, or are you content to be a follower?

- Are there practical matters you should consider? For instance, do you want a job where you have to dress up each day, or do you prefer something more casual?

Preparing answers to critical questions you will likely be asked can help you get ready for an important interview.

- Are you naturally very organized, which would be a necessity for some professions, or do you work best in a less structured environment?

GEEKOID

A common way to help you decide what type of job you would like is to try to describe what you think a perfect workday would be. Another good scenario to consider is what you'd enjoy doing so much that you would continue doing it even if you won the lottery.

- What about the element of time? Do you want a job with a rigid schedule so that you come in and leave each day at the same time, or are you willing to invest more time as needed?

 *Decide what aspects of a job are essential, what parts are desirable, and what parts are negotiable.*

- Where would you like to live? Some types of jobs are more plentiful in particular geographic regions, so that will be a factor.

2. Match your skills and preferences to an industry. After you know your skills, decide what industry will utilize them the most.

GEEKOID

If you can't put your finger on a specific job you'd like to do, try looking through the classifieds at all the different job categories, titles, and requirements. This may prompt you to think of just the right thing for yourself.

Your answers to the questions listed above will help you narrow your choices of which business is best suited for you.

GUERRILLA GEEK

A career coach can help with identifying and exploring career options, making career choices, focusing a job search, and offering support through the job-hunting process. The down side? Expect to pay $50-200 per hour.

- Make logical connections between your preferences and the types of businesses and specific jobs that line up with those inclinations. For instance, if you enjoy doing detailed work, perhaps you should consider accounting or engineering.

If you know you would not want to stay in an office and sit at a desk every day, consider something more flexible such as outside sales. If you do not want to be subject to rigid guidelines about wardrobe, consider a behind-the-scenes job, such as work done over the telephone.

GEEKOID

Decide that job hunting will be your full-time job until you land a position. Devote as much time to your search per week as you would if you were working.

- Having an idea of where you would like to live, even if it is another country, can help you determine which jobs you might consider since some are geographically specific. For instance, if you would like to live near the beach, perhaps you should consider the travel industry.

GEEK🔍ID

The Occupational Outlook Handbook is a nationally recognized source of career information that can be invaluable to job-seekers hoping to identify just the right job for them. It lists hundreds of jobs, the training and education needed for each, the job prospects, potential earnings, and details about the job.

3. Identify specific companies with that industry. Once you know generally the kind of job that suits you, there are several ways you can identify companies within that field that may have job openings.

- **Phone book**—Check the telephone directory under the heading that best describes the type of business you plan to target. There should be several listings. You may call and ask about openings, check to see if they have a web site with job opportunities, or search the internet and/or library for information about them.

- **Want ads**—Most newspapers have want ads divided into specific headings for job listings. Check your local paper to see how its listings are divided and look particularly under the heading that best describes your ideal job. Typical headings include "Clerical," "Sales," and "Professional."

GEEK*Speak:*

"Choose a job you love, and you will never have to work a day in your life."

Confucius

15

- **Chamber of Commerce**—Most chambers of commerce have a listing of local member businesses by category, such as "Publishers," "Health Care," and "Retail." Check to get a list of company names, but also ask if the agency offers a job-posting service. Some chambers accept and circulate résumés to their members, and offer in-house placement services.

GUERRILLA GEEK

Don't let a financial nightmare keep you from getting a dream job! Before beginning your job search, check to see what your credit history looks like.

What does one have to do with the other? Many companies, particularly financial institutions, routinely run a credit check on all potential employees. Applicants with a poor history of fiscal responsibility are not considered for any position. Check ahead of time to be sure your report is good, and that there are no inaccuracies contained in it.

However, you do have rights. Under the Fair Credit Reporting Act, a prospective employer must obtain your permission in writing to access your credit history. If you are denied employment based on your credit history, the employer must give you a copy of the report, along with materials to explain how you can dispute what you believe to be inaccurate information. If you think something negative might be discovered, take a proactive role by explaining it upfront.

- **Internet**—Search the internet by putting in the name of the industry that interests you. You'll get general information about the field, and perhaps even some particular companies.

- **Library research**—Your local library should offer business directories that contain information on local companies. These may help you not only identify where to begin your search, but will also offer vital information to have on hand once an interview/job offer is in the wings.

If you are feeling overwhelmed as you begin to think about finding a job, remember that this is perfectly normal. It may help to know that there's probably more than one job just right for you. That should ease the pressure of finding the one and only.

GEEKOID

The Career Guide to Industries lists information on available careers by industry, including some particulars that you may be wondering about. Here are just some of the things you can find in this valuable resource.
- The nature of each industry listed
- Usual working conditions
- Specific occupations in each industry
- Possible earnings and benefits you can expect
- Employment outlook
- Names of organizations that can offer additional information

GEEKOID

Many recent graduates add to the stress of finding their first job by thinking that they have to find something they can stay with the rest of their lives. Not so! Rather than thinking long-term, think, "What will I do first?"

4. Talk to people already working in your chosen field. Whatever field interests you, you probably already know people doing that type of work.

- Contact people working in your field of interest on a casual basis if you know them personally. Perhaps you know people at your church or in a club that are already doing a job you'd like to have. Ask them what companies you should contact, and ask them for more information about the job.

- If you know them only slightly, contact them at their offices and schedule an **informational interview**. It just means that you make an appointment to talk with someone who is already doing a job that you think you'd like to do. It's also called **research interviewing**. It's an interview you initiate, and then you ask the questions.

 *The purpose of an informational interview is to get information, not land a particular job. You schedule it, and you ask the questions!*

No matter how you know people that you choose to interview, here are some questions you might be interested in asking.

- How did you get interested in this type of work?

- How long have you worked in this job?

- What type of training is required?

- What aspects of this job are most challenging? Satisfying?

- What is a typical day in this job?

- What changes have you seen in this field?

- Will this type of job change in the future?

GEEKSpeak:

"Motivation is a fire from within. If someone else tries to light that fire under you, chances are it will burn very briefly."
Stephen R. Covey

- How great is the demand for people in this occupation?

GUERRILLA GEEK

Job shadowing is a great way to get the feel of a job you think you might be interested in. Don't just talk to someone who's already doing the kind of job you want— go with him or her and be a "shadow" for an entire day. That should give you a good idea of what the job entails; then you'll have a better idea if it's for you.

- What is the best advice you could give to someone starting in this field?

- Are there professional organizations that offer information about this field?

- Has your overall experience in this job been negative or positive?

- If you could change one thing about your job, what would it be?

- Would you choose this field if you could start all over?

- Do you know of job openings in this field? If so, whom should I contact to apply?

5. Begin to look for jobs that fit your criteria. After you have identified the skills and abilities that you have to offer, and what industry can best utilize those, you'll know what kind of job to look for.

Now you're ready to look for specific job opportunities! The next chapter will give you specific places where your dream job might be found.

GEEKOID

Even though informational interviews aren't job interviews, you should still prepare for them. Research the industry under discussion so you'll be aware of critical issues to ask about.

- Make a plan for beginning your job search. It will provide structure and a roadmap for this process.

- Assessing your skills and abilities is an important step in your job search. Not only will this beginning help you identify the right job for you, it will help clarify in your mind what you have to offer an employer.

- Be honest in evaluating your preferences.

- Match your skills and interests to an industry that will utilize them.

- Identify companies in your area that may offer jobs that suit your abilities.

- Talk with people already in your targeted industry to get a good picture of what working in that field will be like.

SEEK AND YE SHALL FIND

Now that you know the kind of job you're looking for, you have to get out there and look for it.

It takes lots of work to uncover job prospects, but the good news is, there are lots of places to look, and as many ways to look as there are places. Here are some of the most common ways. Try them all and you'll find out which works best for you.

1. Networking—Everyone knows people. And those people know other people. Within your circle of acquaintances, there are bound to be people who know about job openings. Consider everyone you meet to be a potential networking contact.

Networking can help you get a job before it has even been advertised or officially listed. Here are some things to remember to help this vital tool work for you.

There is no one perfect way to find a job. To increase your chances of success, try a variety of methods, such as the ones listed below.

If this is not your first job search, do not assume that this one will be like the last one. The methods that were successful last time may not work this time. Be open to new avenues.

GEEKOID

Estimates say that as much as 80 percent of jobs are filled by people who heard about the job informally, that is, from networking.

- Let people know you are looking for a job and ask them to let you know if they hear of openings. In addition to your friends and relatives, include colleagues from previous jobs, alumni from your university, church acquaintances, and people you know in social settings, such as classes you take or sports you play.

- Join professional organizations. Within those ranks, you'll find representatives from numerous companies, and they'll be concentrated within your field. Many organizations offer job-lines or publish newsletters that contain this kind of information.

Remember that networking is a give-and-take concept. Just as you're hoping someone will help you, be ready to offer help to others when you are in a position to do so. The support you offer someone today may pay off when you need help later.

It really is who you know that counts! Networking has been proven to be the number one way that people find a job.

- Diversity counts, too. Cultivate contacts from a variety of companies and job types for a broad cross-section of networks. Associating with people personally and professionally different from you helps broaden your outlook, and introduces you to new ideas and opportunities.

- Learn to ask people about their jobs as a way to make new contacts.

GEEKOID

Be careful not to dominate any conversation with talk of your job search. Do not be in such a hurry to discuss yourself and your skills that you look like a shameless self-promoter.

- Keep an updated file about contacts you have made and the information they offered.

- Make a follow-up file for possible jobs that people indicated might become open at a later date.

GEEKSpeak:

"Don't wait for your ship to come in, swim out to it."

Unknown

- Follow-up on every lead, no matter how tentative they may seem.

 *Know your skills and abilities, and be ready to discuss them if one of your networking contacts asks what you have to offer an employer. There's no use in asking for help unless you know what you'll be offering.*

- Remember to let your original contact know if his or her information produced a promising lead or a job offer. Not only will they need to know that the job opening has been filled, they will appreciate your thanking them for the help.

GUERRILLA GEEK

Don't forget to make other job-seekers a part of your network. Some cities have job clubs or support groups where people meet and share job-hunting tips and information. There's always the chance that a job opening that someone else didn't find to be a good fit would be just right for you. And think about this—who could offer more support for the urgency of your search than someone going through the same thing?

2. **Internet**—Many people have found that this method offers access to job postings they might not normally learn about.

While some surveys indicate that less than 10 percent of students looking for a first job find one on the internet, the advantage is that it is a resource they can use at any time, day or night.

GEEKOID

A recent analysis revealed that the heaviest traffic to job search sites occurs around the beginning of each new year, with people looking for greener pastures as they make a new start.

GEEK☉ID

1st Steps in the Hunt is the name of a web site that offers almost daily updates and newsletters to help with finding a job right for you. Billing itself as "An online column for the online candidate," it offers information about companies with job listings, tools for your search, and numerous other resources.

All types of web sites are available—those offering general job-hunting sites, industry-specific sites, and sites for specific companies.

- Check web sites of specific companies already identified as possible sources of jobs. Many have a section where you can view job openings on their sites.

Check internet job postings frequently, as many are updated daily.

- Check general sites that offer job openings. You can search for jobs on these sites by your particular area of interest, location, and even potential salary.

GEEK*Speak:*

"I know the price of success: dedication, hard work, and an unremitting devotion to the things you want to see happen."

Frank Lloyd Wright

• Many newspapers offer online versions, including their classified sections. Check national and local listings if you are willing to relocate.

3. **Want Ads**—Although it is very easy to check for jobs listed in the local newspaper, it's not the best place to look—statistics say that only about 5 percent of all job openings are listed in the classifieds.

GUERRILLA GEEK

Some job hunting sites require a membership fee before you can access their information. Check the fine print before signing up.

• If this is your primary source for job possibilities, at least respond only to those ads that closely fit your goals. Do not blindly apply to a large number of ads hoping to get lucky with one.

• Broaden your search by checking several newspapers. If you're willing to consider relocation, get copies of out-of-town papers at your local bookstore or newsstand. If hard copies

GEEKOID

Some classified ads have a small section listing job line numbers, that is, phone numbers at particular companies that offer recordings about current job openings. The recordings are usually updated daily, and offer information not only on available positions, but how, where, and when you may apply.

GEEKOID

If you are trying to find a job in a particular niche, search for a newspaper catering to that specialty. For instance, if you are interested in working with organizations that allow expression of a particular faith, check for publications from that religion.

aren't available, check for online versions of papers from the places you might like to live.

4. Professional associations — Joining an association related to your area of interest is a great way to make new contacts. It's like a concentrated network. Most of the people in it will have related jobs in a common industry, so you have a group that's already specialized.

GEEKOID

One place where you might not think to look for a job is the public library. The reference section offers many directories and indexes of all kinds of businesses.

- As a bonus, many professions have member-service arms that not only offer support within a given field, they have active job-hunting services, such as résumé services and specific job postings.

- Check professional journals and newsletters, which often list job opportunities within a specialty. Although there won't be as many actual ads in trade-related publications, those you find will be more specialized, and will allow you to focus your search within your field.

5. Career centers/Campus placement offices — If you're a new graduate looking for your first job, don't overlook your college career center as a source of help.

Not only can your career counselor help identify job prospects, he or she can help you write a résumé and cover letter, practice mock interviews, and keep track of the potential employers you contact. Here are some other services you may be able to tap into:

- **Assessment testing** — Most centers offer tests to help you identify your interests, and then match those with a career objective.

- **Career research** — Centers can offer research, or sources for the information you need, on different careers and companies that might interest you.

GEEKOID

Check with faculty members in your major subject to get some ideas about how to apply your studies in the workplace.

- **Alumni contacts** — Career counselors can put you in touch with alumni working in different fields. This can be a great source to get insider information on a variety of careers, and can be the source for information on jobs available.

GEEKOID

Finding alumni in your field shouldn't be hard. Many universities update alumni information and publish a directory at regular intervals. Sometimes an online version is available.

GEEK○ID

One limitation of campus interviews is that not every industry or type of job is represented. Participation by some companies and industries may be dependent on the condition of the current economy, or other variables.

- **On-campus interviews** — Center representatives may be able to do even more than just offer information about possible openings. They may be able to arrange on-campus interviews with companies that routinely scout for new talent on college campuses.

- **Internships or temporary jobs** — Career centers often have listings of companies or organizations in need of short-term employees. They may not offer the dream job, but they'll offer valuable experience you can list on your résumé. Sometimes, short-term jobs transition into full-time positions.

GUERRILLA GEEK

Virtual job fairs are an extension of corporate web sites, but they offer a face-to-face component to them. They allow job seekers to research companies online before interacting with them in person at an actual job fair. They also offer calendars of upcoming fairs by location and a list of which companies are participating.

6. Job fairs — Job fairs are a common catalyst for getting job seekers together with people looking to hire new employees. They offer employers a chance to meet a high number of prospects in a short period of time.

GEEKOID

Look for representatives who stand in front of the table at their booths. They're likely to be more approachable than those who stand behind their tables and wait for you to make contact with them.

- One obvious benefit to employers is that they get to meet candidates face to face and size them up without having to guess about them from only their résumés.

- Job seekers get a chance to meet a high concentration of employers in one place, and have the added benefit of costing little, if anything.

- Despite the advantages of job fairs, they can be a waste of time and energy if you are not prepared for them. Obviously, you should look your best, since potential employers will evaluate you based on your meeting. But there are several other things you should remember to take with you besides your best smile and your firmest handshake.

GEEK Speak:

"I'm a great believer in luck, and I find the harder I work the more I have of it."
Thomas Jefferson

GEEKOID

Be sure to follow up the job fair with a thank-you to each contact you made. Thank the representative for meeting with you, indicate why you would be a positive addition to the company, ask to meet again, and state when you will call to set up an appointment. Then do it.

- **Résumé** — Bring your résumé printed on quality paper, and bring several copies. If you have multiple versions, bring some of each to fit different opportunities that might be advertised.

- **Letters of Recommendation** — You'll want to take plenty of copies of your letters of recommendation with you in case you meet an employer interested in your qualifications. Don't look unprepared by having run out of copies when asked for one.

GEEK*Speak:*

- **Portfolio** — Your 9" x 12" portfolio will neatly store your résumé and letters of recommendation, as well as notepaper for notes you make after talking with each employer.

"Striving for success without hard work is like trying to harvest where you haven't planted."

David Bly

- **Briefcase** — You'll no doubt be accumulating all kinds of handouts from different employers, and you'll need a place to keep them. A briefcase will present a much more professional

GEEKOID

Don't expect a job offer to be made at the job fair, but it provides a good opportunity to lay the groundwork for a future job.

appearance than the free plastic bags that others might be putting their materials in.

- **Business card** – If you are already employed, have extra business cards to distribute.

7. **Recruiters** — If you need professional help to find a job, find someone who specializes in your field. Check the yellow pages of the phone book for employment agencies.

Here are some important things to remember as you choose the right professional to help you.

GUERRILLA GEEK

To make your business card stand out, consider using something other than the standard 1" x 3" cardstock. Some cards are now being made out of such materials as rubber, wood, or a sturdy fabric. Though pricey, they can distinguish you from the crowd.

- Make sure you deal only with reputable, well-known companies. If you have any questions about their reputation, check with the Better Business Bureau.

GEEKOID

If you're looking in the yellow pages for help in finding a job, don't bother looking under "Recruiters." That'll probably get you a military recruiter (which is fine if you're looking for a military career). If you want a civilian job, look under Employment Agencies.

 *Be sure you understand what fees, if any, apply if you enlist the help of a recruiter.*

• Ask what fees are involved. Most recruiters are hired by employers to fill vacancies so you should not have to pay anything. But ask, just to be sure. Some people find the answer to this the hard way.

• Submit required paperwork to enlist their services.

• Provide the company with a copy of your résumé and contact information.

GEEKSpeak:

"Far and away the best prize that life offers is the chance to work hard at work worth doing."

Theodore Roosevelt

• Be honest with your recruiter about what you will and will not accept. It will save you both a lot of time.

• Let him or her know what ground you have already covered so you do not duplicate efforts.

GUERRILLA GEEK

Don't forget to check with your state's employment agency. Not only does it list state jobs, it will also make referrals for other agencies and companies as well. For instance, some school systems fill non-teaching positions through the state agency. Don't assume that only entry-level jobs are filled this way, either. Many professional positions requiring specialized training are listed here. And it's free!

- Be sure to advise the company of any restrictions on circulating information about your qualifications. Let them know if there are some companies that may not be contacted.

- Check with your recruiter periodically, but don't be a nuisance by calling too often. It is in his or her best interest to let you know as soon as possible if there is an opening for which you might be suited.

- Find out what will happen to your information once you have settled into a job. Be sure you mutually understand if it will be stored, will continue to circulate, or will be deleted from the situation after its designated use.

GEEK◎ID

Before you call, be sure to check the web sites of companies you may be interested in working for. Not only could job openings be listed, but personnel may also be included, which would give you just the right name to call.

 *One of the most important things you can do throughout the job-hunting process is to get and stay organized. You don't want to misplace a piece of paper on which you've written the name of an important contact person.*

8. Cold Calling — Despite the considerable time it takes to develop a list of companies to call, this can be an effective way to locate jobs before they are even advertised. Some people think cold calling shows initiative.

- Start with major companies in the field you've identified.

- Obtain contact names and numbers from the yellow pages, the internet, company web sites, or professional publications.

- Ask to speak with managers in the specific department where you'd like to work.

- If there are no job openings, ask if he or she knows of similar companies that may have openings.

GEEK AT A GLANCE

- Do not rely on any one method exclusively for finding a job.

- Approach each job search uniquely. Do not think that methods that have worked before will necessarily be the key to success this time.

- Try a variety of methods for identifying job possibilities.

- Networking, that is, word-of-mouth contact with other people, is the most effective method for locating job openings.

- Other avenues to the perfect job include the internet, professional associations, career centers/campus placement offices, job fairs, recruiters, and even cold calling.

ROADMAP FOR RÉSUMÉS

Your résumé is the most important document you will need in your job search.

It will likely be the first contact you have with a prospective employer, so his or her first impression of you will come from your résumé.

The primary job of your résumé is to outline your education and work experience, your achievements, and your strengths and weaknesses. But it will reveal much more than that—it will showcase your ability to organize material in a meaningful and logical way, your attention to detail, your communication skills, and whether you care enough to prepare this vital information properly so that it presents you as the professional you are.

Preparing a quality résumé that will be sure to get attention takes work, but the result is worth the investment of time and effort. Here are some ways to make your résumé stand out and attract the

GEEKOID

Some scientific, medical, and academic jobs require a curriculum vitae (CV) instead of a résumé. Some applications for graduate or professional school request a CV, sometimes called vita for short. Like a résumé, it is a summary of one's qualifications and experience, but is much more detailed. Whereas a résumé would be limited to one or two pages, a CV may be anywhere from two to ten pages.

GEEKOID

Many people turn to professional résumé writing services for help in preparing this vital personal marketing tool. Be sure both you and the company are in agreement about how your information will be used, whether it will be stored after your résumé is completed, and whether or not the company may share it with others.

attention needed to get an interview for the perfect job for you.

1. Choose a basic format. You'll need to decide whether you will use a chronological or functional format, or a mixture of the two. Examples of each type are shown. As you prepare your résumé, keep this in mind: Each résumé will be as individual as the

GEEK GLOSSARY

Curriculum vitae means "course of life" in Latin. The plural form is curricula vitae.

person it represents. Samples offered are only guidelines.

- **Chronological** — Actually, reverse chronological might be a better term for this because it lists work experience in reverse chronological order. Beginning with your most recent job and working backwards, list all jobs you have held, being sure to account for all periods of time since you entered the workforce. Even if you have legitimate gaps of time, such as time spent going back to school or raising children, be ready to account for those times if asked in an interview. See the sample for an outline of how this type of résumé should be formatted.

Outline for a Chronological Résumé

Name
Street Address
City, State, Zip
Home Phone (Area Code) Number
Cell Phone (Area Code) Number
E-mail Address

Objective: Briefly state your goal. This may include the immediate particulars of the job you are looking for now, as well as long-term career goals.

Education: Beginning with your most recent education, state the name of the school attended, the degree or certificate you received, your major and minor field, and your GPA.

Experience: Beginning with your most recent job, list the date, job title, company name, general description, and duties of each job you have held.

Honors and Activities: Give the name of the organization, dates of involvement, positions or offices held, and describe the activities.

Special Skills: List specialized knowledge, such as computer programs or office machinery, languages, or other unusual abilities you have to offer.

References: State that references are "Available upon request," then prepare a separate sheet listing the names of several business, academic, or character references.

GEEKOID

The chronological format will work best for those who have several jobs to list. It will not work well for those who have little experience, have large gaps in their work history, or those who have worked for the same company for the majority of their career.

- **Functional** — This format stresses what skills you have, rather than where and when you used them, so it is an obvious choice for those new to working. It's also a good format if you've been out of the job market for a while, and for those seeking to transition from one career or industry to another one. See the outline of information that should be included in a functional résumé.

GUERRILLA GEEK

Résumé software is available to help you prepare this critical summary of your qualifications. Some programs simply offer résumé templates, but others also include information on how to write effective cover letters, interview with confidence, and negotiate for top money.

Outline for a Functional Résumé

Name
Street Address
City, State, Zip
Home Phone (Area Code) Number
Cell Phone (Area Code) Number
E-mail Address

Summary: Briefly state you're an overview of your experience
and qualifications. Mention any specialty you have.

Special   List specialized knowledge up front.
Abilities:

Experience: Beginning with your most recent job, list the date,
job title, company name, general description, and
duties of each job you have held. Also include
special accomplishments during your tenure.

Education: Beginning with your most recent education, state
the name of the school attended, the degree or
certificate you received, your major and minor
field, and your GPA.

Honors and   Give the name of the organization, dates of
Actvities   involvement, positions or offices held, and describe
the activities.

Special Skills: List specialized knowledge, such as computer
programs or office machinery, languages, or other
unusual abilities you have to offer.

References: State that references are "Available upon request,"
then prepare a separate sheet listing the names of
several business, academic, or character references.

GEEKOID

Some experts caution that choosing the functional format may send an automatic red flag to a prospective employer that candidates may be hiding something since they are downplaying their work history. If you choose this format, be careful to be forthcoming about all aspects of your experience and qualifications.

- **Combination** — This combines elements from both formats, listing skills that are relevant to the job search in a special section by function, perhaps in a summary at the beginning of the résumé, while work experience is presented in reverse chronological order. This offers the best of both résumé worlds, and is a popular choice. See the sample outline for information to include in a combination résumé.

GUERRILLA GEEK

The combination format may be especially helpful to the following people:

- Students, new graduates, and entry-level job seekers: the format allows you to emphasize skills rather than employment history.
- Older workers: it allows you to showcase skills and achievements, as well as to indicate your work history.
- Workers with a steady employment history: it allows you to list special skills and then show how those have been acquired/used in your work history.

Outline for a Combination Résumé

Name
Street Address
City, State, Zip
Home Phone (Area Code) Number
Cell Phone (Area Code) Number
E-mail Address

Objective: Briefly state your goal. This may include the immediate particulars of the job you are looking for now, as well as long-term career goals.

Education: Beginning with your most recent education, state the name of the school attended, the degree or certificate you received, your major and minor field, and your GPA.

Honors and Activities: Give the name of the organization, dates of involvement, positions or offices held, and describe the activities.

Work Experience: You may want to offer two sub-headings in this section: Special Skills and Summary. The Special Skills section would highlight specialized abilities, such as knowledge of particular computer programs, and sales or supervisory skills. The Summary would list actual jobs held, beginning with your most recent, and would include dates, titles, company names, and general descriptions of duties performed.

Intrests: You may want to include information about your hobbies, particularly if they are related to your career.

References: State that references are "Available upon request," then prepare a separate sheet listing the names of several business, academic, or character references.

2. Organize your material. Group information that belongs together. Here are some of the things a prospective employer will need to know about you.

GEEK GLOSSARY

The combination résumé may also be called a hybrid résumé because it is a composite of the other two types.

- **Contact information** — Be sure that your name, phone number(s), and e-mail address are prominently positioned on the page. You do not want to be hard to find when an employer wants to call with a job offer!

- **Objective** — This identifies the type of position you are seeking. It should include a broad definition of the job you are looking for, and a mention of the skills that would be utilized in the position. Of course, this portion can be tailored to each employer you contact.

GUERRILLA GEEK

No matter what format you use, list your contact information first so that the various ways to reach you are easily found.

- **Experience/employment history** — Prospective employers want to know what work experience you have already had, exactly what you did, when, and how successful you were. List jobs you have held, including the dates of your employment. Be absolutely certain about the dates, since incorrect dates, even as the result of a simple typographical error, can make your résumé seem questionable. If you are a recent graduate, include internships and assistantships held while you were in school.

- **Skills** — Include particular skills you may have honed, such as computer programs you know, language skills, and other specialized abilities you have developed. Tailor this list as you apply for various positions to list first the skill most relevant to the job for which you are applying.

GEEKOID

Offer more than just job titles and descriptions in your employment history. Present quantifiable results, such as stating the percentage by which sales increased, to demonstrate how effective you were in your previous jobs.

- **Education** — Include schools you have attended, from most recent backwards, plus what degrees you earned there. If you are a

GEEKOID

Don't be offended if you find that the company to which you've submitted your résumé verifies the information you have offered. Most companies do check. The rule of thumb is that the better the job, the higher the pay, the tougher the screening process will be. Not only might the company verify the basics, but, depending on the position for which you are applying, they may even do a criminal background check. It's all part of the process.

GEEKOID

If you have worked for a number of years, do not feel obliged to include every starter job you had when you began your career. Prospective employers are usually only interested in the last ten to fifteen years of experience. On the other hand, if you're just starting your career, include internships and other pre-career jobs, even relevant volunteer jobs, that show where you may have gained valuable experience.

new graduate, include your GPA if it is 3.0 or higher. Mention certifications and professional licenses you hold. If you have been in the workforce for a while, you need not include high school.

- **Awards and affiliations** – Mention professional recognitions and awards, or publications, plus memberships in professional associations. These items will speak about your motivation and dedication, and will also be good conversation starters in an interview.

- **References** – Indicate at the bottom of your résumé that "References will be provided upon request." Do not include

GEEKOID

If your résumé is more than one page in length, it is a good idea to include your name at the top of the second page in case the pages get separated. Also add a brief heading to help further identify it, such as Joe Adams, Résumé, Page 2.

the list of references with your résumé. This will keep your references private until they are actually needed, so that their names and contact information are not casually circulated. This will also make it necessary for the prospective employer to ask you for the references, which will let you know that you are moving to the next step in being considered for employment.

Although you will not send your list of references with your résumé, begin to think about whom you will list, and start to compile a sheet containing their names, titles, and contact information.

GEEKOID

Some employers are reluctant to offer more than basic facts when asked for a reference about a former employee. Some job-seekers may be willing to sign a reference release form promising to release the company from blame in order to get managers to open up about past job performances.

GUERRILLA GEEK

Curious to know what your references are actually saying about you? Professional reference checking firms can find out by contacting everyone on your list to see what is being said when prospective employers call. Most references give glowing recommendations. But sometimes, even though they aren't saying anything negative, they're saying things they intend to be helpful, but are not.

GEEKOID

Asking permission before you list someone as a reference actually serves two purposes. Not only is it an expected courtesy, but it also gives references a "heads up" to let them know they may be asked about you, and allows them the opportunity to think through what comments they will offer.

Be sure to ask permission before offering a name as a reference. Most people are willing to help, but it is an expected courtesy for you to ask their permission before listing them.

If your résumé gains you an interview, do take your list of references to the interview. Then if you are asked for the list, you'll have them available.

3. Prepare the final document to be useful and informative. Here are some tried-and-true things to keep in mind as you organize your information.

GUERRILLA GEEK

Even if you are fresh out of school, include a mixture of references. Offer some academic and personal ones as well, even if you do not yet have work references to offer.

- Be honest. Include everything that can legitimately be included, but do not stretch or embellish the truth. You will be found out, and even one incorrect item will cast suspicion on your application, no matter what position you are applying for.

GEEKOID

If you have worked for only a single company for a number of years, rather than just having the one listing under Work Experience, itemize jobs you have held within the company during that time. Not only will it show off your variety of skills, it will show that your level of responsibility has increased as well.

• Keep your résumé to one page, if possible. This will be easy if you are new graduate. If you have been in the workforce several years, yours will be longer, but do not exceed two pages.

• Be positive about yourself and what you have to offer. Demonstrate faith in your own abilities without being arrogant.

• Offer complete information. Be ready to explain legitimate gaps or omissions.

GUERRILLA GEEK

As important as it is to know what to include in a résumé, it is equally important to know what not to include. Do not offer information about your marital status, number of children, height, weight, age, sex, race, religion, or national origin.

GUERRILLA GEEK

If space permits, you may want to consider including a brief quote from a former employer on your résumé. It will make your résumé unique, and will allow you to slip in a brief recommendation before references are checked. Be sure to include the name and position of the person offering the quote. And, just like with references, be sure to ask permission before using the quote.

- Omit personal pronouns in your résumé. Instead of saying "I did," begin with action verbs, such as "Reorganized the department to increase efficiency by 33 percent."

- Use action verbs to describe your experience, and use a variety of them. Avoid weak, overused words like "worked." Make vivid and different word choices. Edit and edit again to concentrate on substance. No matter what type of job you hope to land, good communication skills will be essential. This is a chance to highlight yours – make the most of it.

GEEKOID

If there are details you are not able to fit into your résumé, consider including them in the cover letter when appropriate.

GEEKOID

Some large companies feed résumés into a scanner for a key word search as part of their processing. Knowing what they are looking for beforehand can help you advance to the next step in getting an interview. If possible, ask a company representative before submitting your résumé if it will be computer scanned. If they are reluctant to say, it probably will be. That means you should get more information about the job.

- Design your résumé in a logical and easy-to-read arrangement. Using the main parts as described above, you should be able to design a résumé that will express your individuality. Pay as much attention to the design as to the content because it must be visually pleasing before it will get a second read. Add bullets or dashes to identify items. Insert spaces to help separate topics.

- Use basic fonts in sizes that will be easy to read. Do not use smaller fonts in an effort to get everything in that you want to include.

- Use spacing and special features such as bolding and italics to highlight your most important qualifications.

- Use your best grammar and spelling. Don't forget to spell check, but remember that even this will not catch legitimate words used out of context. Proofread your résumé several times to catch errors. Lay it aside, and read it again after some time has elapsed.

- Have other people read your résumé and offer their objective opinion of it.

- Print your résumé on high quality paper. Consider using a pastel colored paper for printing your résumé. Do not use bold colors, but a subtle tint may make yours stand out from the crowd.

- If you are mailing your résumé, send it in a 9 x 12-inch envelope, unfolded, instead of in a No. 10 business envelope. When it arrives at its destination, it can be taken out un-creased, and will lie flat (open and readable) on the desk of the person you hope to impress.

GEEKOID

Before you embellish facts to make your résumé more attractive, even in small ways, consider the story of RadioShack's former president and chief executive, David Edmondson, who resigned in 2006 amid admissions that he had "clearly misstated" his qualifications on his résumé. Edmondson's personal lapse cast doubt on the company's credibility as well, which led its board of directors to accept Edmondson's resignation, and begin a search for a new CEO.

- Your résumé will be the most important document you submit to potential employers during your job search.

- Be absolutely truthful with all information you include.

- Your final version should be well organized and easy to read.

- Check carefully for correct spelling and grammar. Errors on your résumé will cast doubt on your qualifications and abilities

- Print the résumé on quality paper.

- If you are mailing your résumé, send it unfolded so it does not arrive creased.

MISSIVE WITH A MISSION

A letter of application, commonly called a cover letter, is essential to accompany your résumé. It will introduce you, explain your purpose for writing, highlight your qualifications, and request an opportunity to meet personally with a potential employer.

The main job of your cover letter is to persuade a potential employer to read and consider your résumé. Along with your résumé, the cover letter will be something on which the potential employer can form a first impression of you and what you have to offer.

 *A cover letter should introduce and compliment your résumé, not duplicate it.*

1. Format your letter correctly. Here are some considerations to help your cover letter do its important job.

GEEKOID

To help personalize letters, write down the description of the job advertised, list the criteria the employer is looking for, and then list the relevant skills and experience you have. Refer to the list as you draft your cover letter.

- Type and print each letter individually.

- Prepare each with a particular recipient in mind.

- Include your address first, followed by the name and address of the company you are writing, plus a contact name if you have it. Try to get the name of the person in charge of hiring. Do not begin letters with "Dear Sir/Madame," or worse, "To Whom it May Concern."

GUERRILLA GEEK

Do not tell your life's story in a cover letter. Be brief and focused.

- Whenever possible, direct letters to a particular person.

- Check the spelling of the name of the recipient. Nothing is as big a turnoff as having your name mangled.

- Include his or her title if possible.

GEEKOID

If you are introducing yourself to someone personally, for instance, at a job fair, you do not need a cover letter. Your verbal introduction will be sufficient.

GEEKSpeak:

"The word that is heard perishes, but the letter that is written remains."

Proverb

GUERRILLA GEEK

Get the name and title of the person to whom you should address your letter by calling the company directly, by checking the company's web site, or from someone you know that works at the company. But if you are not absolutely sure of the name or its spelling, do not use it. Spelling a name incorrectly is a turnoff to many interviewers.

• Limit letters to a single page. Be succinct.

• Highlight skills and experience for a specific application.

• Check and recheck grammar and spelling.

GUERRILLA GEEK

One of the first things that can get your cover letter and résumé taken out of consideration for a job is poor grammar or typographical errors in your cover letter. Make a poor impression there, and it won't matter how sterling your qualifications are.

GEEK◯ID

John Hancock's signature on the Declaration of Independence was so distinctive and prominent that his name has become synonymous with one's signature. It has been immortalized in the phrase, "Just put your John Hancock on the dotted line," which simply means, "Sign here."

 Along with everything else it will do, a cover letter will highlight your communication skills, which will be critical no matter what field you choose.

- Always include your personally written signature at the close of your letter.

2. Carefully consider your content. Here are some particulars to keep in mind as you prepare the body of your letter.

- Tailor each letter individually, mentioning particulars of the company or job advertised. Demonstrate some knowledge of the company you are targeting.

- Make your letter readable. Avoid long sentences and paragraphs. Do not use jargon or trendy terms.

GEEK Speak:

"I consider it a good rule for letter-writing to leave unmentioned what the recipient already knows, and instead tell him something new."
Sigmund Freud

GUERRILLA GEEK

If you are applying by e-mail, you'll still need to send a cover letter with your résumé. You can copy and paste your cover letter into an e-mail, or write it directly in the body of an e-mail message. Include the title of the position for which you are applying in the subject line. If the job advertisement asks you to send your résumé as an attachment, send it as a Microsoft Word document. If attachments are not accepted, paste your résumé into your e-mail message.

- Arrange your points logically, using bullets or other devices as necessary.

- Use active verbs, and active voice.

- Demonstrate enthusiasm and optimism.

GEEKOID

Mention specific skills that may be applicable. There are some skills that will be helpful no matter what type of job you're trying to find, like communication skills, but some jobs are very skill specific. Be sure to include key words that the company might be looking for. For example, management jobs would logically look for words like "managed" and "coordinated."

3. Make sure each part of the letter does its job. Each paragraph has a particular purpose to accomplish as efficiently as possible.

- Your first paragraph should establish a point of contact. Introduce yourself, say who referred you to this company, and mention the ad (and the job listed) that prompted your letter.

- Subsequent paragraphs will highlight the most important points from your résumé. It will show how your education and experience are applicable to the company, and how you could contribute.

Many employers test potential employees by giving them directions for applying for a position, and then seeing how well they follow instructions. Don't fail this first test by doing your own thing.

- Closing paragraphs should politely request an interview at the employer's convenience, and thank the reader for his or her time and consideration.

4. Follow directions precisely to submit your information. One of the most basic ways you can go wrong in applying for a job is to fail to follow directions. The people in charge of hiring know how they want to receive the information you're sending, and will be on the alert for those who don't follow protocol.

- If you are asked to send the information via U.S. Mail, send your cover letter and résumé, plus whatever other information is required, in a neat package to the address provided. Be sure to add plenty of postage. You would not want to be embarrassed to learn that your package arrived with postage due.

• If you are instructed to apply via e-mail, do so at the address provided. Be sure to note whether they receive attachments, or not, and include your résumé accordingly.

• If you are asked to include references, do not omit this vital piece of information, though many companies do not ask for this until the interview.

GUERRILLA GEEK

When sending your résumé in response to an ad, you may have been instructed to include your salary history in your cover letter. Most companies merely ask for this information to determine if your salary expectations are within the range they intend to pay. If you feel strongly that you are not obliged to reveal such personal information (which you probably wouldn't even tell your best friend), there are ways to handle this. One is that you can mention your salary requirement instead of your salary history. Just indicate what it would take for you to accept a new position. Another tactic is to just give a salary range—you can say you made in the "mid-30s." You run the risk of being eliminated from consideration, but if your cover letter is otherwise outstanding, you may get an interview anyway!

- A cover letter should introduce your résumé and make the prospective employer want to read it.

- A cover letter should compliment, not duplicate, your résumé.

- Format your letter correctly.

- Carefully consider what your letter says. It will give an employer his or her first glimpse at what you have to offer.

- Make sure each paragraph in the letter does its job. They should introduce you, tell why you are qualified for consideration, and then request an interview.

- Submit your credentials exactly as you have been instructed by the employer.

SIGNED, SEALED, DELIVERED

When submitting your résumé and cover letter, you can either send it in direct application to specific places, or you can post your résumé online, where an unlimited number of companies will have access to it.

There are a number of factors to consider as you decide how your résumé will be circulated, including the following:

- Do you have the time to get your résumé out to a sufficient number of places yourself?

- Do you have access to names and addresses, or e-mail addresses of those you would like to target?

- Do you need to have a large number of people get your résumé, or is your field so specialized that you should be more selective?

GEEK Speak:

"The reason so many people never get anywhere in life is because when opportunity knocks, they are out in the backyard looking for four-leaf clovers."
Walter Percy Chrysler

Once you evaluate the answers to these questions, you'll know whether to send your résumé yourself, and you'll know whether to send it directly to selected companies, or to send it out en masse.

1. Submitting your credentials directly. You can send your résumé and cover letter directly to specific people in response to particular job openings, or you can send the information in shotgun fashion, to a number of companies.

 *The main advantage to submitting your résumé directly is that you can keep a record of each company contacted, and then you can follow-up with each one.*

In contacting companies directly, you can either submit your material to them electronically, or by good ol' U.S. Mail. There is protocol for doing either one.

Submitting by e-mail — There are specific things to watch out for if you intend to submit your cover letter and résumé by e-mail.

GEEKOID

The advantage of sending your résumé directly to a company is that you can keep a record of when and to whom you sent it, and can follow-up later with the appropriate person.

GEEKOID

Do not rely on e-mail as your only method of contact. If your electronic job application is unsolicited, it may be filtered out by a spam filter, and never even reach your intended recipient.

GUERRILLA GEEK

Before you send your material by e-mail, make sure you have the correct address set up for this. No sense sending your important documents to an address that won't be checked for applications. Many people reject or delete unsolicited mail they are not expecting.

• Be sure to include a subject in the subject line. With the threat of viruses always present, many people are unwilling to open an e-mail without a subject.

• Make your subject attention getting.

• Use an abbreviated business format. Include date, address, name, job title of the person, and a salutation. Do not forget that this is an important piece of communication.

Before submitting your résumé to anyone electronically, send yourself a copy to see how it looks when it is received, so you can check to see if there are format problems caused by transmission.

• Be sure to mention in the first paragraph how you heard about the job opening.

No matter how you choose to circulate your résumé, make sure it is in perfect shape before you send it out. You cannot recall it if you discover it contains a mistake after you've submitted it for consideration.

• Make the inquiry brief and concise.

• Make your grammar and spelling perfect. Proofread carefully. You will not be able to retract the e-mail if you find misspellings after you send it. And your e-mail may be forwarded without your consent, complete with errors.

GUERRILLA GEEK

One advantage you gain by applying via e-mail is that you prove you are computer literate.

• Keep your tone friendly to overcome the fact that e-mails can be impersonal under the best of circumstances.

GEEK☉ID

If you already have a job and are looking for another one, do not send your résumé from your office e-mail. Not only might others see that you are job-hunting, and cost you the job you already have, it will be obvious to the office where you are applying that you are using company time and resources to conduct your job search. Take care of this from home.

- Send a brief reminder in a couple of weeks if you have not received an acknowledgement to your inquiry.

- Read and reread your letter before you click on Send.

 *Remember that your e-mail address will be a contact point for the company to which you've submitted your résumé. Be conscious of how your address looks to others. Don't use something suggestive, graphic, or even childish.*

Sending by snail mail — Some companies still prefer to get applications the old fashioned way. Be sure to take care of all the details to ensure that your package gets there in a timely and correct way.

- Send your résumé printed on good quality paper.

- Include a cover letter to introduce yourself and your application.

GUERRILLA GEEK

Résumé fax companies distribute your résumé via fax to recruiters, and others in a position to hire. There is a fee for this. The fax company will also send your information to specific employers upon your request with a cover letter, also for a fee. A typical deal is that for $20, you could ask that twenty-five employers be contacted.

- Do some research to get a name and title of someone in the position of hiring.

- Send the résumé and cover letter unfolded in a 9 x 12-inch manila envelope. This will allow the materials to arrive without a crease. An added bonus is that they will remain open and readable as they rest on a desk.

GEEKOID

Even if you are sending your résumé in an attachment, you may want to cut and paste a version in your e-mail just in case the recipient cannot open the attachment.

GUERRILLA GEEK

Different versions of your résumé should be prepared so that it is available for sending in a variety of ways:

- A print version, complete with bulleted items and other highlighting devices, should be sent when you mail or hand your résumé to potential employers or recruiters.
- A plain text version can be copied and pasted into online forms or posted onto résumé databases.
- An e-mail version is another plain text copy, but it takes into consideration specific format restrictions, such as line length.

GEEKOID

Résumé posting does not cost the job-seeker anything, but it is used as a source for résumés only by those willing to pay a fee for access. This service offers more exposure than you could probably get by yourself, but its success depends on a couple of critical elements:

1) your résumé must include important key words, and only a given employer will know what those are, and
2) the résumé will be available only to those whose budgets allow them to subscribe.

- Be sure to put adequate postage on your package.

2. Posting your Résumé Online. Thanks to modern technology, you can now offer your résumé for consideration to a large number of potential employers with the click of a button. There are hundreds of sites where you can post your résumé online.

When you post your résumé, you send it to a job board for paid subscriber employers and recruiters to see. After you submit the information, it is the responsibility of those looking to fill positions to find your résumé. This is usually done by their search for particular key words.

- Be sure to keep track of where you post your résumé. This will allow you to follow-up, will prevent duplications, and will be a record of whom you should contact to discontinue circulation of your résumé once you have found a job.

GEEKOID

Not only may you want to protect your identity by posting anonymously to keep your information from being improperly used, you may want to do so to protect your existing job if you are already working. Many employers routinely search for their employees' résumés on posting sites. Imagine what happens when their résumés are found!

• Keep a list of your log-in names and passwords.

 *One advantage that online posting has is that it makes your résumé available twenty-four hours a day to people looking to fill jobs. They do not have to wait until someone is in the office and available to provide it.*

• Consider posting your résumé anonymously. Some sites let you mask your contact information, which lets you control who contacts you. This lets you keep personal information confidential that might make you vulnerable to identity theft. Remember, too, that if you post personal information, you have no control over who gets it and what they do with it.

GEEKOID

Another option to consider for maintaining confidentiality is to set up a disposable e-mail address that you can discontinue at the conclusion of your job search.

GUERRILLA GEEK

Just like the bell that can't be un-rung, you can't un-send information once it has been sent. That's why it is so important to be careful before you ever post your information. Once it is submitted, there's very little recourse if it is abused. If you find that your information has been misused, you may file a consumer complaint with the FTC by calling 1-877-FTC-HELP or by using the FTC's online filing system, located at www.ftc.gov. Click on "File a Complaint Online."

- Thoroughly investigate any job offers that result from résumé posting. Since it is a rather impersonal way of filling a position, you should be sure that a real position exists before you invest heavily in it. Beware of any offer that asks you to transfer money, send driver's license or other ID information, or that mentions third-party payment services.

- Do not include your Social Security number unless you are applying to a state or federal government site.

- Omit the names of references and their personal information when you post your résumé. Choosing to circulate your own information is one thing; choosing to distribute that of your references is something else.

- Check to see if you can delete your information after you have accepted a position. Be sure you understand how long a site says it will keep your résumé. Details should be provided in the site's privacy policy or terms of use section. Your résumé belongs to you, and you must be certain that you retain control of it.

3. **Job banks and job boards** are often hosted by recruiters, employment agencies, and other firms that specialize in the job-search industry.

GUERRILLA GEEK

If you're interested in finding a job in a particular geographic area, check America's Job Bank (also known as America Job Bank or AJB), which connects job seekers not only to national openings, but to state job banks as well. It typically contains close to two million job postings at a given time.

Résumé blasting is the distribution of a résumé to hundreds or thousands of people looking to fill job openings. There are two major disadvantages to this: 1) your résumé will most likely be sent to a lot of people outside your field; and 2) it will no doubt be sent to a lot of people who won't look at it because they didn't request it. But if you're interested in trying this, there are lots of companies online ready to help. Some will even let you target recipients by particular criteria.

GUERRILLA GEEK

Whenever possible, choose to submit your own carefully prepared résumé instead of filling in your credentials with online forms. Using standard forms will have these disadvantages: you probably won't be able to spell-check your information; you'll have to use their format (chronological vs. functional) even if it's not the most advantageous for your information; and it will be a one-time only use (you'll have to do the whole thing over for the next submission).

These sites work like this: Employers post job ads, then job-seekers search the ads and post their résumés in response. Depending on the resources used, either of these may be free, or may require a service fee.

- Industry-specific job boards are becoming more popular as job-seekers use the internet more to target job prospects.

- Note that some job banks and boards charge fees. Be sure you understand the particulars of each site before you enter your information.

GEEKSpeak:

"Know your goal, make a plan, and pull the trigger."
Dr. Phil C. McGraw

- There are several ways you can submit your credentials to companies ready to hire.

- You may submit your résumé directly to companies you would like to contact by regular U.S. Mail, or by e-mail to an address provided for this purpose.

- You may post your résumé online, where potential employers have access to it as a paid subscriber.

- You may apply for jobs listed on job banks and job boards, but be aware that there are fees for some services.

- No matter which method you choose, make sure you follow directions exactly, and understand what you are agreeing to by your participation.

GETTING READY FOR YOUR CLOSE-UP

You've landed that all-important interview! There's much to be done besides just counting the minutes until time for your appointment.

Take time before your interview to arm yourself with as many facts as possible about the company and the position for which you are being considered.

1. Research the company. Find out as much as you can about it. Some things to know would include:

- What it does

- Its size

- How many employees it has

- Its mission statement

- How it has recently performed

- Who its customers are

- Its culture

- Its owner(s)

GEEKOID

If you have learned about this job opportunity as a result of networking, then you probably already know people who work at the company. Don't overlook them as a resource for telling you what the company is like on a day-to-day basis.

- Products and services it offers

- How long it has been in business

- Recent ways it has been in the news

- Branches, locations

Here are some places you might find the information you need.

- Company's annual report

- Literature produced by the company

- Information interview

GUERRILLA GEEK

Informational interviews are a great way to get the low-down on the job you're tracking. For detailed information on this, see an earlier chapter, "In the Beginning".

GEEKOID

There are numerous places where you can find a general salary range appropriate for the job, taking into account your experience and qualifications. Check trade and professional association surveys, Department of Labor Area Salary Surveys, and publications such as *National Association of Colleges and Employers Salary Survey* and the *American Almanac of Jobs and Salaries*.

- Its employees

- Professional journals

- Publications of trade and professional associations

- Library

- Internet

GEEK*Speak:*

"The best work never was and never will be done for money."
John Ruskin

2. Research the job. Although you are going to the interview to learn the particulars about this job opening, there are some things you should know by the time the interview begins.

GEEKOID

If the name of the interviewer is not gender specific, find out whether the person is a man or a woman. If it is the latter, find out whether you should address her as Miss, Mrs., or Ms.

- The specific job title for which you are being considered

- Average salary for this job in the industry—you'll find out from the company how much they're willing to pay for it

- Qualifications expected for the position

- General availability of this type of job

- The name and title of the person who will interview you

GEEKOID

Be sure to carry your materials in a nice briefcase or binder. Women should omit the purse or carry the smallest one you can. One thing you should not take to an interview is your cell phone. If your phone were to ring during the interview, it would tell the interviewer that you did not think the appointment was important enough to merit your undivided attention.

3. Get organized for the interview. There are several things you'll want to be sure to have with you at the interview. Don't rely on your memory to gather them the morning of the interview. Get everything together the night before.

Here are some important documents and other items you may need to get you through the interview.

- Extra copies of your résumé

- A statement about yourself in case you are asked the standard "Tell me about yourself."

- A list of questions you would like to ask. There is no way you will remember these during the pressure of an interview, so write them down.

- List of references

- Sample of your work (such as brochures, reports)

- A notepad and pen or pencil

GUERRILLA GEEK

You cannot pay too much attention to your attire for an interview. Besides wearing your best suit, check to be sure it is good repair, with no loose buttons or threads. If you have bought new clothes for the occasion, make sure all tags have been removed.

- It's not just your important documents you'll need to get together—you have to get yourself and your clothes ready as well.

- Choose your interview clothes with care.

- Select your best business clothing.

- Make sure they are in good repair.

- Check to see if your shoes need a good polishing or brushing.

- Get a quick haircut if yours is looking ragged.

- Think about getting a manicure if there's time.

- Make sure you have plenty of gas in the car so you won't have to stop for it on the way to the interview.

- Confirm the appointment time with the company.

- Make sure you understand directions to the site of the interview.

- Take a trial drive to the site to see how much time you should allow in the morning for the trip, and to see if there are problems that would require additional time, such as construction or detours.

- Get a good night's sleep so you'll be rested.

4. Review your qualifications. This may sound like a no-brainer, but you need to look at your skills and experience from every angle, and be prepared for any question that may be asked about them.

Become an expert on yourself before the interview. Don't be caught off guard by questions about what you have to offer.

Here are some ways to prepare for questions about how much of an asset you can be to a company:

- Review your résumé. You wrote it, and spent time evaluating your own skills and abilities to get it just right. But check to make sure you know what it says if you haven't looked at it in a while.

- Take a look back over dates of previous employment, if any, and think over the jobs you've successfully handled before.

- Think of times you solved a difficult problem or led a project. Even if you have just graduated, and don't have any real job experience, think about times during your academic career when your skills were showcased.

- Identify occasions when you received special recognition for a job well done. Even if you've been in school, that was your job then, and there may have been times when you went above and beyond the call of duty. Perhaps you were given a scholarship, or earned the highest grade point average. Those things speak of motivation and a desire to excel as much as on-the-job performance.

- If you have received special training in your field, review the name of the class(es) and dates. Not only will specialized education show that you are already better qualified than the next guy, it will indicate your willingness to continue to prepare yourself to do the best job possible.

5. **Relax**! Nothing will be gained by getting tense and stressed before an interview, no matter how much you think is riding on it. Take a walk, go to a movie, and get a good night's sleep.

GEEK*Speak:*

"The secret of success in life is for a man to be ready for his opportunity when it comes."

Benjamin Disraeli

AT A GLANCE

- Research the company with which you are interviewing before the interview.

- Find out as much as you can about the particular position under consideration.

- Organize yourself and your materials before the interview so that you present a polished image.

- Review your own skills and abilities, pertinent dates of your employment/schooling, and special recognitions and training you've received.

- Relax so that you do not arrive at the interview stressed and worried.

- Get a good night's sleep. Nothing will prepare you as much as being well rested.

DRESSING FOR IMPRESSING

Clothes make a strong statement about you.
What will yours say at your interview?

Even though a potential employer will know something about you from your résumé, the first thing he or she will notice at your interview will be your attire.

GEEKOID

If you'd like to know ahead of time what the typical dress code for a company is before your interview, you could just call and ask. Some people suggest that you drop by to pick up an application, or other company information, and observe what people are wearing. Of course, make sure you aren't there on casual Friday, when people are not dressed as usual. If there is any doubt, be over dressed instead of under dressed.

1. Dress in your best clothes. You know the saying that "You never get a second chance to make a good first impression!" This is especially true at an interview. Maybe people shouldn't judge you by your clothes, but the reality is that they do, so you need to look your best. Here are some tips for looking like the professional you are.

Even if you are interviewing with a company that allows a casual atmosphere on a day-to-day basis, you should wear your best suit for this important meeting.

• Wear your best business suit. Even if you are interviewing on casual Friday, when employees are dressed in a relaxed way, you must still be in your best clothing.

• Clothes should be pressed and wrinkle free.

By some accounts, a first impression of you is formed within the first twenty-seven seconds.

GUERRILLA GEEK

If you're a man who hates to wear a tie, you can thank Croatians for the invention of what many refer to as a "noose." Around 1635, supporters of King Louis XIV and Cardinal Richelieu came to Paris, and were joined by Croatian mercenaries who wore picturesque scarves around their necks. The style caught on in France, and even soldiers began wearing lace, while officers wore embroidered muslin or silk. Even poor people managed to join in with cotton versions. The expression, "a la croate," soon evolved into a new French word still used today: la cravate.

GEEKOID

Neatness counts. It's not enough to wear the right clothes; you have to have everything in its place and looking its best. Shine your shoes, check your lipstick, and check for loose buttons and threads.

- Dress conservatively. Now is not the time to express your individuality.

- A dark blue or grey suit is always appropriate.

- Make sure all tags on new clothing have been removed.

 *You will probably already be nervous. No need to be uncomfortable as well. Try new clothes on ahead of time. New shoes can be slippery. Check details ahead of time to make sure everything will go without a hitch.*

GUERRILLA GEEK

Part of presenting a nice appearance will be having your interview materials neatly contained and organized. Carry a briefcase in good condition to hold your résumés, references, and pens and paper.

GEEKOID

The research you've done to prepare for the interview can be a big help as you dress for your meeting. With all you know about the company, and the particular job you're applying for, just dress the part. Make it easy for the interviewer to see you slipping into the role you're here to discuss.

• Shoes should be scuff-free and polished, or brushed.

• Make sure clothes fit well. Ill-fitting clothes will detract from a polished image.

• Don't forget your coat. If you're looking for a job in cold weather, your overcoat should look nice.

Here's a quick summary to help applicants of both genders make a good impression.

GEEKOID

Applicants should check themselves in a full-length mirror before going into the interview. Check for a straight tie, clean teeth, and neat hair.

Men

• Wear your best suit.

• Clothes should be stylish—not outdated.

• Even if you've been asked to dress casually, coordinate a sport jacket with your pants.

GUERRILLA GEEK

With today's casual approach to dressing, many men seldom have occasion to wear a tie. But you'll need to wear one to an interview, so here's a quick look at how to tie a standard Windsor knot. It will probably be helpful to look in a mirror as you do this.

- Hang the tie around your neck, with the wide end on your right side. That end should hang down about twelve inches longer than the narrow end, which is on the left side.
- Cross the wide end over the narrow end, then bring it up from behind and through the loop.
- Bring the wide end down, then around behind the narrow end, and up on your right.
- Put the wide end down through the loop you've made, and across the narrow end.
- Turn, and pass up through the loop.
- Complete the knot by slipping the wide end down through the knot in front. Tighten the knot, and draw it up snug to the collar.

- Wear a conservative silk tie featuring dark colors.

- Choose a white or light-colored, long-sleeve shirt.

- Socks and shoes should match, and coordinate with suit.

GEEKOID

Some experts say that not all fields expect applicants to come dressed formally, complete with suit and tie. For instance, if you're interviewing for a job in computer support, khaki pants/skirt and a business shirt/tie may be dressy enough. If you're in doubt, you can either check with the company via phone to find out the standard dress, or go ahead and dress up. It's much better to err on the side of caution. At worst, they'll get to see you at your best, even if you're overdressed.

• Wear socks long enough to keep skin from showing when you are seated.

• Shoes and belt should match.

• Wear a belt or suspenders, not both.

• Limit jewelry.

GUERRILLA GEEK

Women may choose to wear a skirt, or pants, depending on the company and its culture. When in doubt, wear a skirt.

• Facial hair should be neatly trimmed.

• Use aftershave sparingly, and then only in a subtle scent.

• Your only accessory should be your briefcase.

Women

- Wear your best suit.

- Clothes should be conservative, but up-to-date.

- Wear a different suit if you return for a second interview.

- Dress conservatively—no revealing or sexy clothing.

- Clothing should be well fitted—not too tight.

- Blouses should be a conservative color, their patterns should be simple, and sleeves should be at least three-quarter length.

- Skirts should be of moderate length.

GEEKOID

Although it is permissible for men and women to wear a light and subtle fragrance, it is usually best to omit it in case the person you are meeting is allergic to it.

GEEKOID

Men should carry a clean handkerchief in their pockets, and women should be sure to have a tissue handy, just in case a sneeze sneaks up on you at the worst possible moment.

- Wear medium heel shoes—do not wear open-toe shoes.

- Wear pantyhose, making sure there are no runs. Bare legs are not acceptable.

- Keep jewelry to a minimum. Do not wear noisy bracelets or dangling earrings.

GEEKOID

It may be an obvious detail, but don't forget to shower and use deodorant before your big meeting. Don't take chances by showering the night before. Make time for your shower the morning of the interview. And don't forget to check your breath.

- Avoid extreme hair styles.

- Keep makeup simple and as natural-looking as possible.

- Nails should be neatly trimmed. If polish is used, choose a subtle color.

- If you must wear perfume, choose a light scent.

- Omit a handbag if you are carrying a briefcase.

2. **Don't forget grooming.** Appearance is about more than the clothes you wear. Grooming is also a big part of the total impression you create.

GEEKOID

In addition to being careful not to wear strong fragrances, be aware of what you eat ahead of time. Do not eat strong-smelling foods just prior to the interview—their aroma will stay with you, but you may be the only one that does not realize it.

The term "powder room" came from the time when men wore white wigs, and were obliged to go "powder" them.

- Have a current hairstyle.

- Save unusual hairstyles or colors for later.

- Invest in a professional manicure. Nails should be neat and clean, and be of average length. Save exotic nails for another time.

- Wear suitable, and conservative, makeup.

- Leave off jewelry in body piercings, and don't showcase tattoos.

- Don't forget to wear deodorant. The day will be stressful enough without suddenly remembering that you've forgotten this important protection.

GUERRILLA GEEK

Even if you're concerned about your breath, don't eat candy or chew gum during the interview. It will appear to the interviewer that you've taken a casual approach to your time together.

- Limit your intake of liquids in the hours before your interview so that nature doesn't call, and keep calling, during the interview.

 *OK, so you might not think it's anyone's business, but make one last trip to the ladies' or men's room right before the interview so you won't have to excuse yourself later.*

- Check for bad breath.

- Check for dandruff on your shoulders during your last-minute once over.

 **GEEK AT A GLANCE**

- Make a professional appearance by wearing your best business suit to the interview.

- Pay attention to your grooming as well, since it will be an important factor in your overall appearance.

- Take one last look in a mirror before you enter the office for your interview.

- Make one last trip to the restroom before your appointment so you don't have to excuse yourself at a critical point in the interview.

HEY, LOOK ME OVER

When the time comes for your interview, you want to be sure everything goes just right. Most of the things you should remember are common sense. But here are some reminders to help you through this stressful, but essential time.

1. Pay attention to details.
Everything you do, even before the interview has begun, will make a statement about you. Make a good impression before you arrive with these suggestions.

- Call ahead to confirm the appointment. Make sure you have correctly understood the time and day of the appointment, and make plans to leave early.

GEEKOID

Do not go into an interview with the attitude that you are entitled to a job. You may have just earned a college degree, or may have years of experience behind you, but you still have to sell yourself as the right person for the job.

GEEKOID

If you need directions to the interview, get them ahead of time. Do not make a frantic call for help as you search for the company's address. Doing so will indicate a lack of preparation.

GEEKOID

Take the phone number of the company with you in case something unforeseen happens, such as a traffic problem. If something happens to make you late, call to let the interviewer know you have been delayed.

- Dress appropriately. Your appearance will say a lot about you.

- Do not be late. But don't be too early either. If you arrive too early, you'll simply have to loiter and be in the way.

- Stop at the restroom once more as close to your appointment time as possible.

- Do not bring food or drink to the interview. You may be offered a soda or coffee, but you should not bring anything with you.

- Offer a firm handshake when introduced to people.

- Introduce yourself with your first and last name as you offer your hand. Do not call others by their first names unless asked to do so.

GUERRILLA GEEK

If testing will be part of the interview process, here are some things to remember:
- Listen closely to instructions.
- Read each question carefully.
- When taking a written test, write legibly.
- Don't dwell too long on one question.

GEEKOID

Experts agree that much of what a potential employer learns about you during the interview will be from nonverbal communication. Your appearance, your eye contact, how relaxed or tense you seem to be, and even your handshake may be critical indicators on which he or she will form a first opinion.

- Be nice to everyone, beginning with the parking attendant, and including the assistant of the person you are to meet with. You never know who will be critical to your success if you get the job. And be on your best behavior if people come through the reception area and speak with you casually. You never know if those people are more subtle parts of the interview process.

Do not overlook the importance of a handshake. The physical connection you make as you shake hands with someone can leave a powerful impression. Likewise, if your handshake is weak or unpleasant in any way, it can imply negative character, and work traits.

2. Observe good interview etiquette. Put your best foot forward, but try to be yourself, too.

- Wait to be seated until you are asked, but then get comfortable. Make sure you are

GEEK*Speak:*

"Good manners will open doors that the best education cannot."
Clarence Thomas

GEEKOID

Do not take anyone with you to an interview. Even if someone has given you a ride, ask him or her to wait outside.

not staring directly into a light, or are in some other awkward situation.

- Listen, talk, and converse.

- Do not become too casual, even if the interviewer does so. Remember that everything you do is being evaluated.

- Avoid nervous mannerisms. Try to appear calm and collected.

GUERRILLA GEEK

If you're nervous at the interview, remember this: they must already like something about you or you wouldn't be there. Try to tame the butterflies in your stomach and speak up honestly about your qualifications. Don't brag, but be your own advocate.

- Speak clearly and use your best grammar.

- Do not use profanity under any circumstances.

- Avoid the use of slang, such as "cool," or "awesome."

- Speak up so you can be heard, and avoid mumbling.

- Allow the other person to finish speaking before you begin.

GEEKOID

A recent survey showed that many recruiters feel that the worst mistake you can make in an interview is to talk too much. Not only does it not give the interviewer a chance to tell you about the opportunity at hand, it also indicates that you aren't listening very well. Answer questions you are asked, but in general, listen more than you talk.

- Be positive and enthusiastic. If you hear information that is not what you had hoped, ask about it directly when the time is right rather than frowning or appearing annoyed.

- Do not be arrogant and act like you are entitled to a job. Be willing to consider all options. If you are a recent graduate, you will need to be prepared to start at an entry level position.

GEEK*Speak:*

"Opportunity is missed by most people because it is dressed in overalls and looks like work."
                    Thomas A. Edison

GEEKOID

No matter what negative experiences you have had in the past, one of the worst mistakes you can make in an interview is to talk negatively about your former employer. Whatever happened, mention it only if you must, and then say only what you must.

- Watch what your body language is saying.

- Sit up straight in the chair and look confident.

- Make sure your arms aren't crossed in a defensive manner.

GEEKSpeak:

"The most important thing in communication is hearing what isn't said."

Peter F. Drucker

- Don't let your eyes wander as if you aren't paying attention.

- Do not answer by nodding or shaking your head. Answer with words.

- Resist the urge to yawn; the interviewer will take it as a sign of boredom.

GUERRILLA GEEK

If you are asked to complete a job application when you go for the interview, remember that even your handwriting will reflect on you, so be sure to write as neatly as possible. Try not to leave questions unanswered. If there are questions that you consider to be too personal, answer with "Not applicable." Consider answers carefully before you write, and do not cross out answers.

GEEK**O**ID

Hone your interviewing skills by interviewing as much as possible. Even if you aren't sure the job opportunity is for you, not only will it be good practice for you, but you'll have made a new contact, and who knows? The job may be just what you're looking for.

- If you are unsure of an answer, either think about it for a moment, or say that you don't know. Do not shrug your shoulders.

- Avoid mentioning previous experiences that included difficult employers, working conditions, or school experiences.

- Maintain eye contact with the interviewer as you talk together.

- Ask pertinent questions. Here are some things you may want to know about:

    - What are the company's strengths?

    - What is the title of the position to be filled?

    - To whom would you report?

Make notes during the interview to help you remember answers to critical points discussed. This will help you accurately recall information later, and can provide details you'll want to mention in your thank-you note.

GUERRILLA GEEK

Many employers ask behavioral questions during job interviews. This means that rather than focusing on the skills and experience on your résumé, you will be asked open-ended questions that have no one right or wrong answer, but rather, an answer that would tell how you would act in a certain situation. An example would be if you were asked to talk about a particular kind of situation, how you handled it, and what the result was. Although these questions are difficult to prepare for, just knowing to expect them can give you a little edge in handling them. Employers think this kind of question gives them a good idea of how you think, and therefore, how you'll fit into the company.

- Is this a new position, or are you replacing someone?

- Is this position the result of increased growth or expansion?

- What qualities are you looking for in a candidate?

- How important is team work?

- What are the advancement opportunities?

- Are continuing education opportunities offered?

- What initial training is available?

- What is a typical day like?

- What will be the next step in the process of hiring someone?

- When do they expect to make a decision?

If you've scheduled an interview that will be held outside the office, and a meal is involved, refer to the last chapter, "Corporate Courtesies," which includes a section on Meeting and Eating.

- Will you hear from them when a decision is made, regardless of who is hired?

• Be prepared to answer questions as completely as possible, but remember that there are some questions that you should not be asked. In some states, it is against the law to ask questions that invade your privacy. Topics that are off limits include your age, health, marital status, social affiliations, disabilities, arrest record, particulars about military service, religious preferences, and plans for children.

Questions you may be asked may include the following. Take time to think about these standard questions ahead of time and prepare for them.

- Tell me about yourself.

- How did you find out about this job?

GUERRILLA GEEK

With all this to think about, you may think you're the only one on the hot-seat, but the interviewer is under pressure as well, to learn a lot about you in a short period of time, and then to ultimately hire the right person based on his or her impressions. It may help you to know some of the things that an interviewer has to consider during and after the interview:

- What kind of first impression did the candidate make?
- Did there seem to be good chemistry between us?
- What skills does he or she have?
- How could those skills and abilities help our company?
- What are this candidate's strengths and weaknesses?
- How can those be used and improved?
- What significant contributions has he or she made?
- What are his or her ambitions?
- Will he or she be willing to fit into our particular company culture?
- Would he or she be willing to relocate if necessary?
- Does he or she have the ability to manage people, now or later?
- Is this the best person for the job?

- What qualifications do you have that would be appropriate for this job?

- Describe your personality.

- Why did you choose this field of work?

- How and why did you choose your college major?

- Tell me about what your ideal day at work would be.

- What are your strengths/weaknesses?

- What is your greatest fault?

GEEKOID

Low GPA? Don't mention it unless you're asked. Play up other strengths instead. If it comes up, which it probably will, play up your major GPA, which probably applies to the job under discussion anyway. Or calculate your GPA for a specific time. For example, if you had typical freshman grades, but they improved as you began to apply yourself, point that out, and mention how you became a serious student.

• If your grades were really that bad, consider retaking some of the courses with the lowest scores. If that will substantially help your GPA, give it serious thought.

GEEKOID

The Americans With Disabilities Act (ADA) states that an employer with twenty-five or more employees cannot discriminate against a qualified prospective employee with a known disability. The ADA further states that upon hiring a disabled individual, an employer must provide reasonable accommodation unless undue hardship would result.

- Where do you hope to be in five years?

- Why did you leave your last job?

- How do you deal with criticism?

- What is the most important part of a job to you?

- Do you prefer to work alone or as a team?

- How would you handle a difference with a coworker?

When accepting a business card, it is important to observe proper protocol. It is considered impolite to pocket the card without looking at it. Take a moment to read over it, commenting on something interesting like an unusual spelling of the owner's name, or something about his or her title.

- Why do you want this job?

- What can you bring to this job that no other person could?

If improper questions are asked, you have several options.
• You may answer if you do not object to doing so.
• Respond, "Why do you ask?"
• Return to the discussion of relevant qualifications by asking how the question is related to job performance.
• Choose a humorous way to avoid the question.

• Stick to business topics, and do not engage in discussions about religion, politics, or other personal issues.

GEEKOID

Occasionally, you may be offered a job at the conclusion of the first interview if things have gone especially well, and if the company is anxious to fill the position. Although you may be flattered to receive an offer so quickly, it is always better to ask more time to think it over rather than making a hasty decision. Not only will this give you time to consider all the factors involved, but if you want to negotiate any of the terms of employment, you will be in a better negotiating position if you do not seem too eager. Don't let yourself be rushed into this important decision.

GEEKOID

Following the interview, it is a good idea to make notes about details you'll want to remember from the interview for use later. Keep a record of particulars for use in a follow-up letter, and to refresh your memory in case you are asked for a second interview.

- Watch for signs that the interview is over. You do not want the final impression to be that the interviewer couldn't get you to leave!

Do not be the first one to bring up money. Not only will it show your hand if you appear too concerned with it, but it will also make you seem more interested in the money than the job. When pressed to declare the salary you expect, offer a range, not a definite number.

3. Conclude the interview appropriately. Once you realize that it is time to leave, tie up loose ends using these guidelines to help you finish.

- Wait for the interviewer to indicate that the meeting is over. Besides a verbal indication that you are finished, he or she may close

GEEKOID

A recent survey found that 65 percent of employers expect a thank-you note following an interview. About half of that number found an e-mail note to be acceptable.

GEEK⊙ID

A thank-you note can help distinguish you from other applicants in the mind of a prospective employer. Even if you don't get the job you're after this time, the thank-you note can leave a positive impression that can bring you to mind for another opening later.

his notebook, stand up, or ask if you have any final questions.

- Let the interviewer know if you are interested in remaining in consideration.

- Express your appreciation to the interviewer for having taking his or her time to meet with you.

GUERRILLA GEEK

What if you don't want the job? You'll still want to thank the interviewer for his or her time, but be honest in stating that you don't think you and the job are a good match. It may seem awkward, but the interviewer will no doubt appreciate your honesty, and knowing that you handled this situation professionally might even bring you to his or her mind for another job for which you're better suited.

• Ask if there is anything else the company needs to know about you before choosing a candidate for the position.

• Ask for your interviewer's business card. This will give you a name and title for follow-up.

If you interviewed with more than one person, you must send separate and individually-tailored letters to each person.

 *The most important thing in an interview is to be honest. Admit when you don't know an answer or if you're asked something you hadn't anticipated.*

• Ask what the next step in the process will be.

• Ask when a decision will be made, and if you will be notified when a decision has been made.

• Offer a concluding handshake and leave.

GEEKOID

If one of your networking contacts is responsible for getting you the interview, and especially if it results in a job, don't forget to send a letter to the contact who helped you. Even if you don't get a job offer, it can let your network contact know that you are still receptive to news of other available positions.

GUERRILLA GEEK

Even if you learn immediately that you will not be offered a job, or receive a call saying that you were not chosen for the position, you can still use a thank-you letter to your advantage. Thank the interviewer for taking his or her time to meet with you, and express interest in being considered for future positions.

4. Follow-up properly. Although you can breathe a brief sigh of relief after the interview, your job is not done. There are several things to do as you wait to see the outcome of your meeting.

- Send a thank-you note. This is the perfect final touch to an interview. Some interviewers even think it may be sent as an e-mail. Either way, you should thank your interviewer for taking his or her time to consider your qualifications. This is not optional.

- Address the letter to the person who interviewed you, including his or her properly-spelled name, and a proper title. If you failed to get a business card with this information on it, call the company and ask for it.

 *Timing is everything! A thank-you should be sent the day following the interview.*

- Address the interviewer with an appropriate title of courtesy, such as Mr., Mrs., or Miss. Do not use his or her first name unless you have a prior relationship, or unless you were specifically asked to do so.

- Keep your note brief and concise.

- Use your best grammar and spelling skills. Even though the first impression you made was the most critical one, the one you leave now will be a lasting one.

- If sending a letter or note, use quality paper.

- Thank him or her for taking time to meet with you.

- Recall the interview. Make reference to something particular you discussed.

- Connect yourself to the job. Remind him or her of how your qualifications will help the company.

- Indicate a subsequent contact. Let the interviewer know that you look forward to discussing the job further.

- Conclude the letter with any number of closings, such as "Sincerely," or "Yours truly."

 Do not stop looking for a job just because you've had a good interview that looks promising. You don't have a job until you have received and accepted a firm offer.

- Call if you have been asked to do so. If you have been asked to call the interviewer on a certain day after the interview, mark your calendar and do so as you were asked. You will show that you can be depended on to follow instructions in a timely manner.

- Ask when you might expect to hear from them. If the company has not reached a decision when you call, ask when a decision will be made.

GEEK AT A GLANCE

- Pay attention to details right from the start of the interview.

- Observe good interview etiquette during the meeting.

- Conclude the interview appropriately.

- Send a thank-you note the next day to the interviewer. This is a must.

- Follow up properly by calling or checking with the interviewer promptly according to any agreement you made for this.

WHEN OPPORTUNITY KNOCKS

The ideal result of your preparation and interviews will be a job offer (or maybe even more than one).

You might be tempted to think your work is done once you receive a job offer, but if so, you'd be wrong. There's still much to do in considering the offer.

Here are some important factors to consider as you think about any job offer that you receive:

1. What do your instincts say? — Does it feel like the right thing? Don't take a job because you think your parents or family expect it. You'll be the one spending time on the job, and life is too short to be miserable for the sake of accommodating someone else. If you find that you're dreading the job already, admit that you really don't want it, and turn it down.

When extending a job offer, most companies will allow you time to think about the offer and get back to them with an answer. If a company presses you for a decision on the spot, it may be a red flag for you to proceed with caution.

Think carefully about your true feelings toward the job. Don't ignore your instincts.

2. Is the money adequate? — Prior to getting the actual job offer, you should not mention money specifically, but you may confirm a general range for the position under discussion. Set a budget for yourself so you know what you will require to meet monthly expenses. If you find that the job pays considerably less than you actually need to live on, then you know up-front that it will be a waste of your time and the employer should continue dealing with others.

Here are some guidelines to help you know if the salary being offered is appropriate for the job under consideration.

- What is the industry standard for this position? You should have researched this in preparation for the interview.

- What is the lowest you can consider, taking into account your financial obligations and living expenses?

- If you feel that the salary is too low, what factors would justify your being paid more?

- If the salary is lower than you'd like, but you'd really like to get the job, remember that it may

GEEKSpeak:

"Do not hire a man who does your work for money, but him who does it for love of it."
Henry David Thoreau

GEEKOID

Wait until you have a firm job offer, preferably in writing, to begin negotiation. Until that time, everything is tentative.

GEEKSpeak:

"All I've ever wanted was an honest week's pay for an honest day's work."
Steve Martin

GUERRILLA GEEK

Do not fail to consider that there is more to the value of the job than just the salary. Here are just some of the perks that may make up the total package.

- Medical insurance
- Life insurance
- Dental insurance
- Disability insurance
- Health club membership
- Retirement program
- Clothing allowance
- Child care
- Educational reimbursement
- Travel opportunities
- Paid vacation days
- Paid holidays
- Relocating expenses
- Free or paid parking

still be worthwhile, especially if it will get your foot in the door at a company you'll be able to grow with.

There might also be extras like health club memberships, a clothing allowance, educational reimbursement, or travel opportunities. If these or other items are included, estimate a monetary value for them, and consider the entire amount to fully appreciate the offer.

When considering the total job offer package, carefully evaluate benefits included to get a complete picture of the offer.

If the job is really something you'd like to consider, but the salary is below the standards you've found in your research, consider making a counter offer. The possibility of such a response may have even been anticipated and factored into the original low offer.

Not only will you want your starting salary to be something you can live on, but subsequent pay raises will probably be figured on a percentage basis, making the beginning number doubly important.

GEEKOID

If you are in the early stages of your career, you may think you have no say-so when and if you get that prized job offer. But that's not so. Employment should be a mutually rewarding arrangement.

3. **Duties**—Make sure you understand clearly what the duties of the job will be. Do the primary responsibilities sound interesting, or do you think they'll bore you to tears? Assuming you'll be working full-time, you'll be spending about two thousand hours a year on the job. Decide if you will enjoy spending that much time on the job as it's been presented.

GEEK*Speak:*

"The test of a vocation is the love of the drudgery it involves."
Logan Pearsall Smith

4. Company culture—By the time you receive a job offer, you probably know a lot about the company. Not only will you have visited there and learned about it from the interviewer, but you have located more objective information during your research to prepare for the interview.

GEEK*Speak:*

"Going to work for a large company is like getting on a train. Are you going sixty miles an hour or is the train going sixty miles an hour and you're just sitting still?"

J. Paul Getty

Factor all that information together to help you decide if you and the company offering you the job will be a good match. Is this a company you like? Do the employees like each other, or did you sense tension when you visited? Granted, you've only had a little time to make that judgment, but if you feel that the people you've met have been stressed, there may be a reason. Listen to your intuition.

Here are some questions to ask yourself to help you evaluate what it would be like to work at a particular place:

- How were you treated when you arrived for the interview?

- Does the office appear to be clean and well organized?

- Were employees busy?

- Were there offensive elements in the office?

- Did you have a chance to hear any employees comment on the office?

• Do you like the size of the company?

• Do most employees stay with the company long?

5. **Company size**—How will the company's size affect your opportunities there? Smaller companies may offer broader authority and responsibility, plus more access to top management. Larger companies may provide more avenues for advancement, but on-the-job opportunities may be more limited.

Don't rule out small companies because you think they don't offer the opportunities a larger company might. Not only are chances for getting hired greater in a small company, but once you're in, your scope of responsibilities may be wider.

Consider logistics about the company, too. Is it nearby, or would you be required to relocate now or later? All those factors should be a part of the equation.

6. **Opportunities for advancement**—If you are starting in an entry-level job, you hope that you won't stay there forever. Ask about opportunities to grow in the job and be promoted. If you've been in the workforce a while, you'll be interested to know how the level of the job compares to

In addition to opportunities for advancement, you may want to ask about opportunities for additional training and development.

previous jobs you've held. Sometimes a lateral move is wise strategically, but you'll want to know about the advancement as well.

7. Location of job—Will relocation be required now or later? If so, will the company help with moving expenses? Also, consider any critical factors that might be dependent on location, such as health issues.

8. Hours required—Most jobs have regular hours, say forty hours a week, but some require overtime. Some demand overtime at regular intervals, such as at month end, or during inventory. Will you be able to accommodate night, weekend, or holiday work if asked to do so? Take into account how extra or irregular hours will affect your personal life.

GEEK Speak:

"The only job where you start at the top is digging a hole."
Anonymous

9. Your supervisor—Even if your primary interviews have been through a human resource professional, you will have no doubt met the person you'll be working for by now. What was your impression? Is this someone you could work for and get along with every day? What is his or her place within the organizational chart, and what will be your place in relation to it?

GEEK Speak:

"It's not the hours you put in your work that counts, it's the work you put in the hours."
Sam Ewing

121

GEEK AT A GLANCE

- Here are some important considerations in evaluating a job offer.

  - What is your instinctive reaction to the offer?

  - Does the money seem right for the job and for you personally?

  - Do the duties seem reasonable and within your ability to do?

  - Is the company culture one with which you'd be comfortable?

  - Are there opportunities for advancement?

  - Are you compatible with the supervisor?

- Even if you are new to the job market, do not think you have no grounds on which to negotiate or make a counter-offer. Employment should be a mutually agreed-upon arrangement.

YES, NO, OR MAYBE

Once you've received and considered a job offer, you must respond to it.

There are three ways you can respond to it: accept, decline, or ask for more time.

1. Accepting an offer — If you've decided to accept the offer you've received, here are the steps you should take.

- Notify the employers with a phone call to accept. Make every effort to speak with your contact person instead of leaving a message.

 *Once you decide to accept an offer, call the company as soon as possible to let them know of your decision. Be sure to call within the time frame the company requested.*

- Follow up with written acceptance. You may send an e-mail if asked to do so.

- Mutually decide on a day for you to begin your new job.

GEEKSpeak:

"There is no substitute for hard work."
Thomas Edison

- Now that you have accepted a position, you may stop your search efforts.

- Notify other prospective employers that you must withdraw your name from their consideration.

GUERRILLA GEEK

What if you are notified that you didn't get the job? If you get a letter saying you were not chosen, immediately call and ask what you were lacking. Knowing that will help you recognize any weaknesses you may have.

If incorrect information was responsible for your not getting the job, calling will give you the chance to clear up any misunderstanding that may exist. It won't help with this job, but may allow you to be considered for later positions.

If there was another problem with your application, you can isolate it and correct it. For example, if you've received a poor recommendation, perhaps you can contact the person who offered it and see if there was a misunderstanding.

If you find that you were the company's second choice, call the company again in a few weeks to restate your interest in working there. It could be that the first choice didn't work out, but at the very least, it will keep you in consideration for other positions.

- If you are changing jobs, notify your current employer that you will be leaving, and decide on how much of a notice you will be required to work.

2. Declining an offer — Sometimes the right answer is "No." For those times, you'll need to know just the right way to handle your response.

- Notify the employer of your decision as soon as it is made. Make a phone call, and then follow-up in writing.

 *Declining an offer may not be easy, but you should let the employer know as soon as possible if you've decided to say "Thanks, but no thanks."*

- Do not say anything negative, even if something less-than-positive has led to your decision to decline the offer.

- Thank the employer for his or her time and consideration. Every person you meet in your job search has the potential to be a vital connection for you at some point in your career. Don't burn bridges.

3. If you are undecided — If you are not ready to accept or reject the offer, you still must get in touch with the company at the time you promised you would.

GEEKOID

Not only should you let the company know immediately if you have decided to decline a job, just out of courtesy, but they will need to begin immediately to interview or contact another candidate.

GEEKSpeak:

"Whatever you can do, or dream you can, begin it. Boldness has genius, magic, and power in it."

Johann Wolfgang Von Goethe

GEEKOID

If you are offered a job and ask for time to think it over, most companies expect you to give an answer within a week, though some will allow an entire week. A few may even be willing to wait longer. Be sure to contact the company with your answer at the agreed upon time. If you must ask for an extension, be sure to state why you need more time, and set a specific time to let them know your decision.

• Thank the employer for the offer.

• Indicate that you are still undecided.

• Ask if you may have more time to consider the opportunity.

 *If you are undecided, and ask for more time to consider the offer, make your decision as soon as possible. Give the company a date by which you can let them know something.*

• Let the company know if there is additional information you need.

• Indicate when you will give them a decision.

• Get in touch with the company on the date you have agreed upon.

GEEKOID

Do not let a job offer get away because you let the deadline go by without making the decision.

• Do not ask for an additional extension of time.

 GEEK
AT A GLANCE

• Once you have considered an offer, you must respond by accepting it, declining it, or asking for more time to consider it.

• If you accept, call to accept the offer, then follow-up with your acceptance in writing.

• Once you accept, do not continue to interview with other companies.

• If you decline, let the interviewer know as soon as your decision is made.

• Thank the interviewer for his or her time, and for the offer.

• If you are undecided, ask if you may have more time to consider the offer.

• Call with a definite answer as soon as possible, and do not ask for an additional extension.

IT'S NOT EASY BEING GREEN

You've landed the perfect job, and now it's your first day. You want to lay the groundwork for a good relationship with your new employer, and your new co-workers.

That means you'll have to pay attention to how you conduct yourself, especially on this critical first day. You've used your best manners to put your best foot forward in your job search, and it is no less important to use those same good manners as you begin to work.

How you get along with people at work is always a critical factor because employers want to hire people who know how to conduct themselves.

GEEKOID

Studies have found that "soft skills," or how you get along with people and handle various situations, are actually more important than your technical skills.

Because your knowledge of proper behavior will be such an important part of getting and keeping a good job, here are some things you should know about how to behave like the professional you are in a variety of situations.

First impressions will be critical your first day on the job. If your behavior is not up to what it should be, you may create a poor impression that will haunt you later.

- Be on time, but not too early. You probably won't have a key to the office yet, and you do not want to have to wait till someone comes to unlock the office/building.

- Dress appropriately for the company and your job. You should have already been advised about any dress code that you'll be expected to follow.

GEEKOID

The most important thing you can do on your first day is to exhibit a positive attitude toward your new job, and a willingness to learn.

GUERRILLA GEEK

Knowing how to make introductions properly can be a valuable business skill to master that will put people at ease. Always remember to introduce a lower-ranking person to a higher-ranking person. For example, if your CFO is Mr. Perry, and you are introducing the new receptionist, the correct introduction would be "Mr. Perry, I'd like you to meet Margaret Scott." If you forget a name while making an introduction, don't panic. Admit your lapse in memory, and ask that the person refresh your memory.

- Introduce yourself to everyone you meet and offer a warm handshake.

- Call people by their first names only after you are asked to do so.

- Make an effort to learn what each person does and how he

GEEKSpeak:

"Politeness and consideration for others is like investing pennies and getting dollars back."

Thomas Sowell

or she fits into the organization. This will be essential later, but in the beginning, it can help you learn about the people and the company as well.

- Be polite to everyone. You never know who may be critical to your success.

 *Learning names and faces can help you begin to feel at home.*

- Be careful of forming alliances quickly. Give yourself time to learn if there are people that you should steer clear of.

- Do not talk about how you did things at previous jobs you may have had. If another job was so great that everyone should copy it, you should have stayed there.

 *Don't talk about past jobs negatively, but neither should you talk about them like they were perfect. They weren't.*

GUERRILLA GEEK

Business etiquette differs from social etiquette in that it has its origins in the military, with emphasis on rank and hierarchy. That means that people of both genders are treated equally, with preferential treatment being given to those with seniority. Social etiquette is based on the concept of chivalry, with gender-specific rules and guidelines.

- Learn the location of critical areas, such as restrooms, break rooms, and the supply/copy area.

- Give yourself a break and allow for mistakes. You are bound to forget some names in the early

GEEK*Speak:*

"Blessed is he who has found his work; let him ask no other blessedness."

Thomas Carlyle

GEEK**OID**

Although profanity in the workplace is so common that it has been called "a barometer of corporate culture," a recent poll reveals that even though many people admit to being regularly guilty of using it, 75 percent of woman and 60 percent of men are offended by swear words interjected into everyday conversation.

days, and you may do some things wrong as you learn. Accept this as a normal part of adjusting to a new situation.

- Be cautious in divulging personal information about yourself. You may regret having volunteered what should be kept private.

GEEK*Speak:*

"Always bear in mind that your own resolution to success is more important than any other one thing."
Abraham Lincoln

- Watch your language! Do not use profanity or coarse words in your conversations.

- Organize your work area and keep it that way to reflect a professional attitude toward your work.

- Set up your voice mail, e-mail, and any other form of communication you will need to personalize.

- Observe your co-workers to see how much conversation is normal as the business day progresses.

- Keep a notebook handy to jot down information that you may need later.

No one can be expected to remember everything, especially amid the stress of a new job. Keep notes to help you remember people and things that you'll need to know later.

- Listen more than you talk. You can learn a lot about your new employer just by paying attention to the routine conversation of others.

- Show appreciation for everyone's efforts to help you make a smooth transition.

- Even though you may not be constantly busy on your first day, do not be a clock watcher, ready to bolt to the door at quitting time. Be available to stay late if necessary to spend time learning some aspect of your new job.

- First impressions will be critical to your first day on the job. Your behavior on this important beginning will set the tone for a successful tenure in the company.

- Make an effort to meet and learn the names of your new co-workers, as well as a general idea of what each does.

- Do not talk negatively about previous jobs or co-workers; by the same token, do not speak of them as the ideal that your current employer should emulate.

- Make notes about information that you may need later, until your routine becomes familiar.

CORPORATE COURTESIES

Now that you've made an impressive start with your new job and your new co-workers, you'll want to maintain your reputation for being a courteous co-worker by observing a few common sense guidelines in the office.

Not only should you want to be kind to your fellow employees, but remember this: if you ever decide to change jobs, you'll need references from this job to put you in good stead for a better one.

 Good behavior on the job is especially important if this is your first job right out of school. It can set the tone for your entire career.

There are general things that are expected if you are to get along every day with your coworkers. Here are some things to help you go from being a good employee to a great one.

- Fulfill your job responsibilities. You probably received a job description during your interview, so do what you were hired to do.

- Be on time for work every day. Do not try to cheat the clock by routinely slipping in at the last minute, and being the first one to leave each day.

- Do not loiter in commonly shared areas like the break room or the hallways. Even if you don't have anything to do right then, you might disturb others who are busy.

- Avoid office gossip.

- Show respect for co-workers by not talking about them to others.

- Receive office guests at the time of their appointments, and do not keep them waiting for you. While some people may feel that keeping people waiting is a show of power, it actually looks like a mismanaged schedule.

> ## GEEKOID
>
> Men and women are equal in the workplace, so women should extend their hands to offer a handshake and prevent confusion about it.

- Avoid expressions of affection toward co-workers, except during exceptional situations such as when expressing sympathy or congratulating him or her on a special achievement.

- Do not engage in office romances. There are too many things that can go wrong, and then you'd still have to work together afterwards. Dating co-workers can also create awkward office

GEEKSpeak:

"If you are going to achieve excellence in big things, you develop the habit in little matters. Excellence is not an exception, it is a prevailing attitude."

Charles R. Swindoll

GUERRILLA GEEK

Growing your own geeks? In an effort to solve the shortage of qualified workers, some large companies are trying to solve the problem by interesting even youngsters in their companies by sponsoring career-driven summer camps. Companies such as IBM, Texas Instruments, and Boeing, promote their industries by offering exposure to everything from engineering to aerospace.

situations, and discomfort among others in the office.

- Be considerate in using common office equipment such as copiers and fax machines. Do not monopolize them.

GEEK *Speak:*

"Whoever one is, and wherever one is, one is always in the wrong if one is rude."
Maurice Baring

- Congratulate others on promotions and recognitions.

GEEK GLOSSARY

The word **etiquette**, which means card or placard, originated in the French royal courts in the 1600s and 1700s. Strict rules regarding behavior were posted on cards in highly visible places for all to see and observe.

GEEKOID

Although we occasionally refer to "giving the cold shoulder" when we mean to slight a person with a snub, the origin of the term is food-related. Supposedly, during the Middle Ages in Europe, to "give the cold shoulder" meant that guests who had outstayed their welcome were literally served a platter of cooked but cold beef shoulder. He or she was supposed to take the hint at that time, and leave.

- Offer to help when others are overwhelmed by too much work and not enough time.

- Acknowledge all co-workers when you see them, even if there are some that aren't your favorite.

- Respect and comply with the chain of command.

- Give credit where credit is due. Always mention those that have helped when a project goes well.

GEEK*Speak:*

"My grandfather once told me that there were two kinds of people: those who do the work and those who take the credit. He told me to try to be in the first group; there was much less competition."

Indira Gandhi

- Respect the property of your co-workers. Do not open their mail, e-mail, or listen to their voice messages.

- Ask permission from the owner before borrowing any item.

Now that we've covered some general do's and don'ts, let's look at some particular ways and situations where it will pay to make the extra effort to be considerate as you work.

At Your Desk
- Dress in compliance with company dress code.

- Eat at your desk only if company policy allows it, but do not consume foods with strong odors that would bother other people nearby.

- Speak in a moderate volume in your personal and phone conversations so you do not disturb others.

GUERRILLA GEEK

Cubicle courtesies are a must in an office with open work spaces. Treat these areas with the same respect you would afford an enclosed office—do not enter without permission, and do not disturb conversations or work that may be in progress. Be careful not to casually discuss confidential information while working in this type of area that offers almost no privacy.

GEEK*Speak:*

"Researchers at Harvard say that taking a power nap for an hour in the afternoon can totally refresh you. They say that by the time you wake up, you'll feel so good, you'll be able to start looking for a new job."

Jay Leno

- Try to keep your desk as organized and neat as possible, especially if it is in a place where others frequently see it.

- Keep the volume on your phone ringer at a volume that will not disturb other people.

- Remember that your desk/workstation is for business, and do not overload it with personal mementos.

Courteous Conferences

- Be at the meeting a few minutes before its scheduled starting time.

- The chairperson should decide the particulars of the meeting, such as when and where it will be held. These details should be confirmed as much as possible with those who will attend to be sure there are no conflicts.

- Arrive prepared by bringing materials you promised to provide, as well as basic supplies such as a notebook and pen.

- Offer an agenda to attendees if you have been in charge of planning the meeting. This will allow them to follow the meeting as it develops, and anticipate business that will be brought up.

GEEK**O**ID

If your work calls for you to travel or even just communicate internationally, be aware that rules of etiquette differ from one country to the next. Do not expect other cultures to do things the same way we do. No matter what your dealings—whether making appointments or giving gifts—be sure and check the norms for a particular culture before you act.

- Turn off your cell phone so that its ringing does not disturb the meeting, which deserves your full attention.

- Introduce yourself to other attendees that you may not know.

- Before sitting, check to be sure that seats have not been assigned for any reason.

- If you are expecting a call that cannot be taken later, alert the other participants ahead of time that you will excuse yourself when the call comes.

- Those in charge should keep the meeting within the time frame set ahead of time.

GEEK*Speak:*

"There are few, if any jobs in which ability alone is sufficient. Needed, also, are loyalty, sincerity, enthusiasm, and team play."
  William B. Given Jr.

• Be prepared to speak when called upon, but do not interrupt other speakers to express your thoughts. Do not monopolize the meeting once you have been given the floor to speak.

• Stay for the entire meeting unless you absolutely must leave early, and even then, do so only occasionally. Do not make a habit of it.

The first e-mail was sent in 1971 by a man named Ray Tomlinson. The text of the message announced the creation of this form of communication, and included instructions on how to use the @ character.

• Be sure that others who did not attend the meeting, but who will be affected by its results, know of the business conducted.

If you see BCC on your desktop, and don't know what it means, that's because you're too young to remember it. BCC stands for Blind Carbon Copy. It was used in the days when carbon paper was used with typewriters to make multiple copies of a document for distribution. If your copy had BCC at the bottom, that meant your copy was "blind," that is, unknown to the other recipients.

GUERRILLA GEEK

It's not always your electronic behavior after you're hired that's important. Some companies now include in their pre-hire background checks a peep into the candidate's online behavior. They check out what a job seeker puts online for all the world to see. The findings may even be a critical part of whether an applicant is considered for a job. A recent survey showed that of all the companies surveyed, 77 percent had found online content that concerned them about the job seeker. In 35 percent of the cases, the material was objectionable enough to disqualify them from consideration.

Netiquette

- Do not type in all caps. That's the equivalent of screaming at your reader. It will also make you look like you're lazy for not taking time to correct it.

GEEKOID

Rules for social and business behavior have been around a long time. The first known etiquette book was written in 2400 BC by Ptahhotep. America got into the act when a fifteen-year old George Washington wrote his *Rules of Civility*, but the most popular "first" was Emily Post's 1922 volume, *Etiquette in Society, In Business, In Politics, and at Home.*

• Take time to put in a subject. In this day of unwanted, and harmful, e-mails, many of which come anonymously, people are wary of opening documents they don't recognize. If you want yours read, put in a subject.

• Don't add colored text, background colors, etc. Stick to plain text.

According to a recent study, there are about 1.1 billion e-mail users worldwide. That's about one in every six people on the earth.

• Do not forward chain letters, jokes, or other unimportant e-mails to all your friends and co-workers. They don't have time to read them, and even if they did, it shouldn't be on company time.

• Give co-workers advance warning if you are going to send very large documents electronically. Compress large files before sending, if possible.

GEEKOID

Among the numerous things invented by Thomas Edison was the word "hello." He coined the word, derived from "holler," in 1889. Prior to the common use of "hello" to answer a phone, people just picked up and said "yes."

- Avoid sending personal information in e-mails. Once an e-mail leaves you, you have no control over who gets a copy. Your information could end up being used, and misused, by people who shouldn't even have it.

- Do not use Return Receipt Request for each e-mail you send. Trust people to read their mail and respond.

- Do not write an e-mail in anger.

GEEK Speak:

"Rudeness is the weak man's imitation of strength."

Eric Hoffer

- Always check your grammar and spelling before sending documents. Don't expect your spell check to catch everything. It won't alert you to legitimate words used out of context.

On the Phone Again

- Identify yourself when answering your own phone.

- Smile as you answer. Although the caller cannot see you, your expression will be revealed in your tone of voice.

GEEKOID

When Alexander Graham Bell tried to sell the rights to the telephone patent to the Western Union Telegraph Company for $100,000 in 1876, the company's president, William Orton, turned him down, saying, "This electrical toy has far too many shortcomings to ever be considered a practical means of communication."

- If answering someone else's phone, answer by saying their name and office.

- Identify yourself immediately when you are the one making the call.

GEEK*Speak:*

"People have been known to achieve more as a result of working with others than against them."

Dr. Alan Fromme

GEEK**OID**

When leaving a message, play it back and listen to it when you are given the option. This will allow you to make sure your recording accurately conveys what you intended.

- If you must put a caller on hold, check back with him or her periodically to say you are still trying to help with the call.

- Do not transfer a call without letting the caller know you are doing so.

- When taking a message, be sure to accurately get the caller's name and number, plus jotting down the time and date of the call.

GEEK**OID**

The current thriving economy has allowed businesses to make the most of the business lunch and dinner. More than ever, companies are choosing to make restaurants their meeting places where they sell products and close important deals.

GUERRILLA GEEK

If you are conducting business during a meal, always treat your server with respect. If you are on a job interview, it will be a good sign to your interviewer. If you are already employed, it will be expected. Do not use terms like "honey" and "dear," or other terms of familiarity.

- If you reach a wrong number, apologize, and hang up. Do not just hang up without letting the other party know what happened.

- Speak clearly and concisely when leaving a message.

- Do not eat, drink, or chew gum while you are on the phone.

- Always return calls when you are asked to.

- When you will be out of the office for an extended period, leave a recorded message to let callers know when you will return, and whom they may contact if they need help before that time.

- If you need to break away from a call for any length of time, give the other party the option of holding or being called back.

GEEKSpeak:

"To fulfill a dream, to be allowed to sweat over lonely labor, to be given a chance to create, is the meat and potatoes of life. The money is the gravy."

Bette Davis

GEEKOID

If you are in doubt about what utensil is used for what dish, watch and follow the lead of others. Even if none of you are perfectly correct, at least you'll all be doing the same thing.

- End your call with "Goodbye" so that both parties know the conversation has concluded.

Meeting and Eating

- Be on time when you have agreed to meet at a restaurant to conduct business.

- Put briefcases and purses on the floor by your chair, not on the table.

GEEKOID

Once you have used silverware, it should not be placed on the table again. Allow it to rest on your plate when it is not being used.

- There is no place for elbows on the table, no matter how informal your get-together.

- When seating is decided, take into account left-handedness and right-handedness as a practical matter.

If you will be interviewed over a meal, remember that general interview rules apply. Be prompt, dress properly, and come prepared.

GEEKOID

If you have questions about items on the menu, do not hesitate to ask your server. It is part of his or her job to provide information.

- Place your napkin on your lap as soon as you sit down, and then do not put it on the table again until the meal is completed.

GEEKSpeak:

"A dinner lubricates business."
 Lord William Stowell

- Be careful about ordering alcohol. Do so only if others are, and even then, be careful not too drink too much and exhibit inappropriate behavior.

- Wait until everyone arrives before you order.

- Know the layout of a basic table setting and each utensil's proper use. Start on the outside and work your way "in."

GEEKOID

The custom of clinking glasses after a toast was originally practiced to drive away evil spirits that may have inhabited the dwelling.

Salad fork – If a salad will come before the meal, the salad fork will be found to the left of the dinner fork. In very formal meals, a salad may be served after the entrée, in which case the salad fork will be to the right of the dinner fork.

149

GUERRILLA GEEK

To deal with gristle or a piece of bad food in your mouth, remove it with the same utensil you used to put it in your mouth. Once removed, place it on the edge of your plate, covered with some other food.

Dinner fork – This will be the largest fork. It is used for the entrée and side dishes.

Soup/fruit spoon – If soup or fruit is served as a first course, this utensil will be in the outermost position to the right of the plate.

Dinner knife – This will be the largest knife, and is intended to be used with the entrée. It will be found just to the right of the plate.

Butter knife – This small utensil will be found across the edge of the butter plate. Replace it there after each use.

Dessert fork/spoon – If these are not brought with the dessert, you may find them placed together above the dinner plate.

• Order with care. Choose foods that can be easily managed.

GEEK Speak:

"You moon the wrong person at an office party and suddenly you're not 'professional' anymore."

Jeff Foxworthy

- Order moderately-priced items if you are asked to order first.

- Do not blow on your food to cool it.

- Keep pace with others and finish about the same time.

- Eat some of your order, even if you don't like it.

- Do not put too much in your mouth at one time.

- Avoid personal grooming at the table. Do not comb your hair or floss your teeth. If those things are necessary, excuse yourself and go to the restroom.

If olive oil is served with your bread, pour a small amount into your bread plate and dip broken pieces of bread into it before eating. Do not dip into other people's bread plates.

- Remain calm if you spill a drink, or have another type of accident. Apologize and ask your server to help you clean up the mess.

- Use your utensil, not your fingers, for most foods. Here are some items that may properly be managed with fingers.

  Artichoke – This is actually the leaf-enclosed flower bud of a plant in the thistle family. To eat it, pull a leaf off, dip it, scrape the flesh from the base of the leaf with your top teeth, then discard the leaf on the plate provided for that purpose.

GUERRILLA GEEK

When you are finished, indicate this by placing your fork and knife diagonally across your place. Place the knife and fork side by side, with the sharp side of the knife blade facing inward, and the fork, tines down, to the left of the knife. Place them securely so they do not slide off the plate.

Asparagus – This may be eaten with the fingers as long as it is not covered with sauce, or it is not too mushy.

Barbecue – Unless you're in a formal setting, where this probably won't be offered, you may eat it with your hands. But if you're say, at a casual company function, eat with your hands, but be careful about letting it get too sloppy.

GEEK Speak:

"People are always good company when they are doing what they really enjoy."
Samuel Butler

Bread – Bread should always be broken—never cut with a knife. Tear off a piece no bigger than two bites worth, and eat that before tearing off another.

Cherry tomatoes – Except when served in a salad, these are intended to be eaten with your fingers. Remember that they squirt, so choose one you can eat whole.

Chicken wings – Always use your hands.

GUERRILLA GEEK

Here are some final don'ts about dining and doing business.

- Don't turn your wine glass upside down if you do not want wine. Simply say "No thank you" when it is offered to you.
- Don't salt and pepper your food before tasting it. Give it the benefit of the doubt. If it's fine as is, you might ruin it by rushing to judgment.
- Do not dunk your food.
- Do not talk with your mouth full. Take manageable bites.
- Don't clean your plate. It will look like you've never eaten before.
- Do not ask for a doggy bag.
- Don't drink too much.

Chips, French fries – You will probably never see these served in a formal setting. But you may see them at casual business meals. When you encounter them, they may be eaten with the fingers. If the fries are thick steak fries, they may be eaten with a knife and fork.

Corn on the cob – This food may always be eaten with fingers, but you probably won't encounter it at a formal meal. Even if you're offered it on the menu, and even if it sounds wonderful, another choice would be more easily, and neatly, managed. If

GEEK*Speak:*

"Good manners: The noise you don't make when you're eating soup."

Bennett Cerf

you choose this item, use corn holders, and eat in a pattern, not randomly.

Egg rolls – Use your hands for eggs rolls and fried wontons. If they're large, you may also use a knife and fork.

Hors d'oeuvres, Canapes, Crudités – Almost everything served at a cocktail party or during a pre-mail cocktail hour is intended to be eaten with the fingers.

Pizza – Cut into manageable bites, and eat with the fingers.

Sandwiches – Most sandwiches are intended to be eaten with the fingers

GEEK⊙ID

In ancient times, eating with the left hand was considered to be profane. The left hand was thought to be guilty of doing "polluting actions" that the right hand did not do. Lefties had to eat with their right hands or starve.

unless they are open-faced, or saturated with sauces.

Shrimp – Use your hands to peel the shrimp out of their shells. If they're served without the shell, use a fork.

Small fruits or berries on the stem – Eat strawberries with the hulls on, cherries with stems, or grapes in bunches with your fingers. Otherwise, use a spoon for small berries.

- Unless time is critical, wait until the meal is complete to introduce the talk of business. If you are at a job interview that includes a meal, the topic at hand will be introduced by the interviewer at a time of his or her choosing.

- Be sure to thank your host or hostess for the meal before you leave.

GUERRILLA GEEK

At very formal dinners, you may be offered a finger bowl at the end of the meal. These are small bowls of water for rinsing the fingers. Often, there will be a slice of lemon floating in the water. Delicately dip your fingers in the water, dry them on your napkin, and then set the bowl to the side of your plate when you are finished.

- Use your best manners everyday with co-workers. They deserve your consideration, and the reputation it earns for you will set a positive tone for your entire career.

- Be on time for meetings, and do not leave early unless there is an unforeseen emergency.

- Be aware of proper protocol for sending e-mails. Do not use all caps, do not forward chain letters or similar "junk" mail, do not read other people's e-mail, and never write an e-mail while you are angry.

- Smile when you are on the phone. Your attitude will be reflected in your voice.

- Try to help people when they call, but refer them to someone else if needed. Let them know they are being transferred before you conclude your portion of the call.

- Many important meetings, including job interviews, are conducted over a meal. Make sure you know basic dining etiquette so you can conduct yourself well on these occasions.

- Do not be too casual during the meal. Remember that business etiquette is still expected.

- If you are unsure of what to do in a particular situation, use common sense, and remember to treat others fairly. The best rule really is to treat others as you would want them to treat you.

INDEX

A

American Almanac of Jobs and Salaries, 78

America's Job Bank, 74

Americans With Disabilities Act, 106

Aptitude tests, 11

Assessment tests, 30

B

Business cards, 34, 106

C

Campus interviews, 31

Career coach, 14

Career counseling, 11, 30

Career diary, 12

The Career Guide to Industries, 17

Classified ads, See Want ads

Cold calling, 37

Company culture, 119-120

Cover letter, 57-65

Credit history, 16

Curriculum vitae, 39

D

Dressing for interview, 85-94

E

Etiquette
Conference, 140-142
E-mail, 142-145
First day, 129-134
Interview, 97-113
Introductions, 130
Meeting and Eating, 148-155
Telephone, 145-148
Workplace, 135-156

F

Fair Credit Reporting Act, 16

H

Hobbies, 11

I

Informational interviews, 18, 20, 78

Internet job postings, 26-28

Internships, 31

Interviews, 77-113
  Conclusion of, 108-113
  Dressing for, 85-94
  Etiquette during, 97-113
  Follow-up, 111-113
  Informational, 18, 20, 78
  Preparation for, 77-83

J

Job banks/boards, 74-75

Job clubs, 26

Job fairs, 31-34
  Virtual, 31

Job offers, 115-127
  Consideration of, 115-122
  Response to, 123-127

Job shadowing, 19

L

Letter of application See Cover letter

Letter of recommendation, 33

N

National Association of Colleges and Employers Salary Survey, 78

Networking, 23-25, 77, 110

O

The Occupational Outlook Handbook, 15

P

Personality tests, 11

Professional associations, 24, 29, 79

R

Recruiters, 34-36, 99

References, 48-50, 80

Reference checking firms, 49

Reference release form, 49

Research interview, 18

Response to a job offer, 123-127

Résumé, 33, 35, 39-55, 80
    Chronological, 40-42
    Combination, 44-45
    Format, 40-45
    Functional, 42-44
    Posting online, 71-74
    Submission of, 65-76
    Writing services, 42

Résumé blasting, 74

Résumé fax companies, 69

Résumé software, 42

Résumé writing services, 40

S

Salary history, 63

Salary ranges, 78, 115-118

Skills
    Identifying, 9-13
    Matching to an industry, 13-14
    Soft, 11, 129

State employment agency, 36

T

Testing, 11

V

Virtual job fairs, 31

W

Want ads, 28-29